My Story K

my FAMILY my LIFE

Authors: Craig Froman
& Andrew Froman

Master Books Creative Team:

Editor: Willow Meek

Design: Terry White

Cover Design: Diana Bogardus

Copy Editors:
Judy Lewis
Willow Meek

Curriculum Review:
Kristen Pratt
Laura Welch
Diana Bogardus

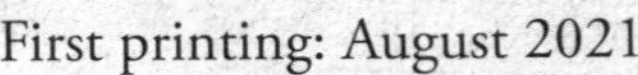

First printing: August 2021

For information write:
Master Books®, P.O. Box 726,
Green Forest, AR 72638
Master Books® is a division of the New Leaf Publishing Group, Inc.

ISBN: 978-1-68344-270-7
ISBN: 978-1-61458-784-2 (digital)

Images are from shutterstock.com, Getty.com, PD-US, and The Great Passion Play.

Printed in the United States of America

Please visit our website for other great titles:
www.masterbooks.com

ABOUT THE AUTHORS:

Craig Froman is assistant editor at New Leaf Publishing Group and author of *Passport to the World* and *Children's Atlas of God's World.* He has a bachelor of arts in business administration and a master's degree in education. He is the proud father of Andrew Froman, whom he helped homeschool through high school. Craig is pictured here standing by the Monument to the Discoveries in Lisbon, Portugal.

Andrew Froman studied at John Brown University in Arkansas, with an emphasis in psychology and history. As a student, he traveled with a study abroad program through Switzerland, Germany, Austria, and France. He is the proud son of Craig Froman, and they enjoy walking and talking about life whenever they get together. Andrew is pictured here standing by Neuschwanstein Castle in Germany with some friends from his study abroad trip.

Dedication: We truly hope this series will be a blessing to you and your family, inspiring joy in learning and love for the people of the world that God loves so deeply.

— Craig & Andrew

Quest 1 – My Family & Culture **Page 15**

Quest 2 – My Citizenship **Page 77**

Quest 3 – My Geography **Page 139**

Quest 4 – My Financial Things **Page 203**

Appendix

Using This Teacher Guide

Features: The suggested two-day schedule enclosed has easy-to-manage lessons that guide the reading, worksheets, and all assessments. The pages of this guide are perforated and three-hole punched so materials are easy to tear out, hand out, grade, and store. Teachers are encouraged to adjust the schedule and materials needed in order to best work within their unique educational program.

Teaching My Story: In the front of this book you will find a special section on the eight areas of intelligence that is woven through the My Story Series. Will students be learning about facts and figures, exploring history and culture, discovering new words and languages? Yes, to all this and more! Yet this series was not meant to look or feel like a typical social studies course. They were designed to meet the various developmental needs of each child in a unique way. Some call these the eight areas of intelligence or eight learning styles.

Approximately 30 minutes per lesson, two days a week, for 36 weeks

Answer keys are included

Worksheets are included for each lesson

Flashcards are included that can be used to quiz students

Designed for kindergartners in a one-year course

Course Description: This is a unique kindergarten social studies course. Social studies for kindergarten typically include introductions to family and culture, what it is to be a good citizen, basic geography and understanding simple maps, and basic economics and the value of things. For this course, it also includes a better understanding of God's love for us, our families, and other people in the world. The core of the course is built on the foundation of family, neighborhood, and church, and it encourages families to explore the world together through four quests, to understand it better from God's perspective. It is designed to make weekly learning fun and interactive!

Course Objectives: This course will focus on:

- homes and families around the world
- helping children think about their lives from their immediate families and beyond
- learning about people in other parts of the world through similar and different foods, rules, and celebrations
- learning passages of the Bible

As students work through the course, the teacher will be helping them create a story book of their year so they can reflect on who they are in their eyes and in God's eyes. The primary purpose of the course is to introduce God's world to children so they are familiar with more of the world when they are done. The focus is not on rote memory or memorization of facts and figures.

Charting Your Course

The following are the teaching elements you will find in *My Story K*. As always, teachers are free to adapt the studies to the abilities and skills of each student:

Narration is a form of instruction where students talk or tell what they've learned in a lesson or respond to information they have learned and apply it to life situations. Talk Time is often started with a question, either about the lesson or about a student's life experience. This is such an important time for the teacher to listen to the words and hearts of the students.

Go time!

This is the lesson introduction for the first day of the week. It sets the tone for the rest of the things that will be studied.

Language 07:00 time!

Each lesson includes a phrase for "thank you" from a different language (36 in all). Children are at a prime developmental level for language learning at this age. These are also found in the back of the book on the Language Time Flashcard pages that can be pulled out. Students are encouraged to color in the countries where the language is spoken on the continent maps provided in the back of the book. Teachers will need to help the students find the countries.

Nine verses throughout the Bible are provided, one for each lesson in each quarter, as a way for younger children to see God's heart, to see what His Word teaches us about Him and ourselves, and to help us live more wisely. These verses are repeated through the quests in order to encourage Scripture memorization. They are also found in the back of the book on God's Scripture Time Flashcard pages that can be pulled out.

Picture time!

Artistic expression at any age creates an emotional connection to the learning experience. Have fun and color or create!

From parents to firefighters to road construction workers and more, people in our communities do so much and work so hard to help our world be better. They are God's blessings!

During each week, students will look for a **yellow highlighted** word on the lesson pages for their Word Collector. The highlighted words are related to important vocabulary words in the lesson, and all have a flashcard in the back of the book that can be cut out and saved.

At the end of each lesson, there is a time for the child to help create a My Book, which is a fun way to record a bit of themselves in words and images as a record of their life for this vital year. Weekly prompts create a story that includes birth dates, favorite foods, and more. Teachers may help by being the student's scribe. Tear out to save!

At the end of each quest, we will be looking at the different types of foods people around the world eat. More specifically, we will be learning about staples. Staples are food items that we eat every day, sometimes at every meal. And then there will be a special recipe for you to celebrate with!

Quest Collector Card!

Each Quest Collector Card has clue questions to keep students alert to what they're learning. Make sure to read these before the quest begins. Tear out each card as you begin a new quest!

Eight Areas of Intelligence (Multiple Intelligences)

Let's face it. We all learn in different ways. You may be naturally talented in playing basketball or in any sport that you pick up. However, maybe you can't carry a musical tune. We all have different talents with which God has blessed us. Some things come easier than other things. The theory of multiple intelligences was constructed by a developmental psychologist named Dr. Howard Gardner. He is a prolific author in educational theory. His most noted work, *Frames of Mind: The Theory of Multiple Intelligences*, suggests that there are at least eight different types of human intelligence, or ways of understanding the world around us. In his book, he discusses how most individuals rely on one or two dominant intelligences. In our quest to acquire knowledge to understand our heavenly Father and the world around us, it is important to strengthen all of our levels of intelligence (from *Elementary Anatomy* by Dr. Lainna Callentine).

The eight areas of intelligence are the following:

1. INTRAPERSONAL (independent learner, strong self awareness) understands personal thoughts and feelings well. These are the people who are introspective. They tend to understand themselves well. They analyze their thoughts and feelings. They enjoy individual activities. They are "self wise." Teaching element(s) focused on this area:

   Go time! and My Book time!

2. VERBAL-LINGUISTIC (writing, reading, listening) uses language to present ideas and express feelings. These are the people who love to color the world through their words. They think in words. They learn best by writing, reading, and speaking. They are "word wise." Teaching element(s) focused on this area:

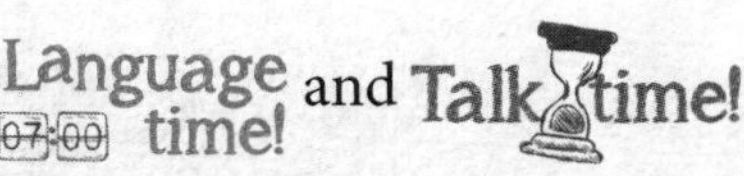

3. VISUAL-SPATIAL (visualization, pictures, colors) creates visual images to communicate the world. These are the people who think in shapes, colors, and images. They can see the spatial relations in things and know that things will fit just by playing with them in their minds. They are "picture wise." Teaching element(s) focused on this area:

   Picture time! and Go time!

4. MUSICAL (sound, song, music) is moved by rhythms and music to express thoughts and feelings. These are the people who can pick up a tune naturally. They hear it once and instantly "get it." They are aware of rhythms and learn best with activities that involve music. They are "music wise." Teaching element(s) focused on this area:

   Language time! and God's Scripture time

5. BODY-KINESTHETIC (physical experiences) experiences the world physically through touch. These people have good physical awareness. They can bound on the playground from apparatus to apparatus like a billy goat scaling the side of a mountain. They are the ones who need to move, and they benefit best through hands-on discovery. They are "body wise." Teaching element(s) focused on this area:

   Picture time! and Go time!

6. INTERPERSONAL (interacts with others, discuss) understands thoughts and feelings of others. These people enjoy working in groups and playing on teams. They enjoy their experiences best with others. They are the "people wise." Teaching element(s) focused on this area:

   Helping hands time! and Talk time!

7. LOGICAL-MATH (patterns, questions, experiments) uses reason and logic to understand the world. These people are rational intellectuals. They can see the abstract. They work best with numbers or patterns. They are "logic wise." Teaching element(s) focused on this area:

   Go time!

8. NATURALIST (experiential) understands the patterns of nature. These people are acutely aware of the many patterns in nature. They learn best when activities involve animals, plants, and the outdoors. They are "nature wise." Teaching element(s) focused on this area:

   Go time! and Food Time

It can be very rewarding to capture your student's interest based on his or her particular learning style and then stretch him or her to develop skills in the other intelligences. God calls us at times to step out of our comfort zone. The more we follow Him and allow that discomfort to occur, the more He can use us.

Suggested Two-Day Schedule

Date	Day	Assignment	Due Date	✓
		First Semester-Quest 1		
Week 1	Day 1	Read Introduction • Pages 13–14 • Remove the first Quest Collector Card Pages 15–16 • Complete Lesson 1: Exercise 1 • Pages 17–20	8-11	✓
	Day 2	Complete Lesson 1: Exercise 2 • Pages 21–22, 265	8-12	✓
Week 2	Day 1	Complete Lesson 2: Exercise 1 • Pages 23–26	8-16	✓
	Day 2	Complete Lesson 2: Exercise 2 • Pages 27–28, 266		
Week 3	Day 1	Complete Lesson 3: Exercise 1 • Pages 29–32		
	Day 2	Complete Lesson 3: Exercise 2 • Pages 33–34, 267		
Week 4	Day 1	Complete Lesson 4: Exercise 1 • Pages 35–38		
	Day 2	Complete Lesson 4: Exercise 2 • Pages 39–40, 268		
Week 5	Day 1	Complete Lesson 5: Exercise 1 • Pages 41–44		
	Day 2	Complete Lesson 5: Exercise 2 • Pages 45–48, 269		
Week 6	Day 1	Complete Lesson 6: Exercise 1 • Pages 49–52		
	Day 2	Complete Lesson 6: Exercise 2 • Pages 53–54, 270		
Week 7	Day 1	Complete Lesson 7: Exercise 1 • Pages 55–58		
	Day 2	Complete Lesson 7: Exercise 2 • Pages 59–60, 271		
Week 8	Day 1	Complete Lesson 8: Exercise 1 • Pages 61–64		
	Day 2	Complete Lesson 8: Exercise 2 • Pages 65–66, 272		
Week 9	Day 1	Complete Lesson 9: Exercise 1 • Pages 67–70		
	Day 2	Complete Lesson 9: Exercise 2 • Pages 71–75, 273		
		First Semester-Quest 2		
Week 10	Day 1	Remove the second Quest Collector Card • Pages 77–78 Complete Lesson 10: Exercise 1 • Pages 79–82		
	Day 2	Complete Lesson 10: Exercise 2 • Pages 83–84, 274		
Week 11	Day 1	Complete Lesson 11: Exercise 1 • Pages 85–88		
	Day 2	Complete Lesson 11: Exercise 2 • Pages 89–90, 275		
Week 12	Day 1	Complete Lesson 12: Exercise 1 • Pages 91–94		
	Day 2	Complete Lesson 12: Exercise 2 • Pages 95–98, 276		
Week 13	Day 1	Complete Lesson 13: Exercise 1 • Pages 99–102		
	Day 2	Complete Lesson 13: Exercise 2 • Pages 103–104, 277		
Week 14	Day 1	Complete Lesson 14: Exercise 1 • Pages 105–108		
	Day 2	Complete Lesson 14: Exercise 2 • Pages 109–110, 278		

Date	Day	Assignment	Due Date	✓
Week 15	Day 1	Complete Lesson 15: Exercise 1 • Pages 111–114		
	Day 2	Complete Lesson 15: Exercise 2 • Pages 115–116, 279		
Week 16	Day 1	Complete Lesson 16: Exercise 1 • Pages 117–120		
	Day 2	Complete Lesson 16: Exercise 2 • Pages 121–122, 280		
Week 17	Day 1	Complete Lesson 17: Exercise 1 • Pages 123–126		
	Day 2	Complete Lesson 17: Exercise 2 • Pages 127–128, 281		
Week 18	Day 1	Complete Lesson 18: Exercise 1 • Pages 129–132		
	Day 2	Complete Lesson 18: Exercise 2 • Pages 133–137, 282		
		Second Semester-Quest 3		
Week 19	Day 1	Remove the third Quest Collector Card • Pages 139–140 Complete Lesson 19: Exercise 1 • Pages 141–144		
	Day 2	Complete Lesson 19: Exercise 2 • Pages 145–146, 283		
Week 20	Day 1	Complete Lesson 20: Exercise 1 • Pages 147–152		
	Day 2	Complete Lesson 20: Exercise 2 • Pages 153–154, 284		
Week 21	Day 1	Complete Lesson 21: Exercise 1 • Pages 155–158		
	Day 2	Complete Lesson 21: Exercise 2 • Pages 159–160, 285		
Week 22	Day 1	Complete Lesson 22: Exercise 1 • Pages 161–164		
	Day 2	Complete Lesson 22: Exercise 2 • Pages 165–166, 286		
Week 23	Day 1	Complete Lesson 23: Exercise 1 • Pages 167–170		
	Day 2	Complete Lesson 23: Exercise 2 • Pages 171–172, 287		
Week 24	Day 1	Complete Lesson 24: Exercise 1 • Pages 173–176		
	Day 2	Complete Lesson 24: Exercise 2 • Pages 177–178, 288		
Week 25	Day 1	Complete Lesson 25: Exercise 1 • Pages 179–182		
	Day 2	Complete Lesson 25: Exercise 2 • Pages 183–186, 289		
Week 26	Day 1	Complete Lesson 26: Exercise 1 • Pages 187–190		
	Day 2	Complete Lesson 26: Exercise 2 • Pages 191–192, 290		
Week 27	Day 1	Complete Lesson 27: Exercise 1 • Pages 193–196		
	Day 2	Complete Lesson 27: Exercise 2 • Pages 197–201, 291		
		Second Semester-Quest 4		
Week 28	Day 1	Remove the fourth Quest Collector Card • Pages 203–204 Complete Lesson 28: Exercise 1 • Pages 205–208		
	Day 2	Complete Lesson 28: Exercise 2 • Pages 209–210, 292		
Week 29	Day 1	Complete Lesson 29: Exercise 1 • Pages 211–214		
	Day 2	Complete Lesson 29: Exercise 2 • Pages 215–216, 293		

Date	Day	Assignment	Due Date	✓
Week 30	Day 1	Complete Lesson 30: Exercise 1 • Pages 217–220		
	Day 2	Complete Lesson 30: Exercise 2 • Pages 221–222, 294		
Week 31	Day 1	Complete Lesson 31: Exercise 1 • Pages 223–226		
	Day 2	Complete Lesson 31: Exercise 2 • Pages 227–228, 295		
Week 32	Day 1	Complete Lesson 32: Exercise 1 • Pages 229–232		
	Day 2	Complete Lesson 32: Exercise 2 • Pages 233–234, 296		
Week 33	Day 1	Complete Lesson 33: Exercise 1 • Pages 235–238		
	Day 2	Complete Lesson 33: Exercise 2 • Pages 239–240, 297		
Week 34	Day 1	Complete Lesson 34: Exercise 1 • Pages 241–244		
	Day 2	Complete Lesson 34: Exercise 2 • Pages 245–246, 298		
Week 35	Day 1	Complete Lesson 35: Exercise 1 • Pages 247–250		
	Day 2	Complete Lesson 35: Exercise 2 • Pages 251–252, 299		
Week 36	Day 1	Complete Lesson 36: Exercise 1 • Pages 253–256		
	Day 2	Complete Lesson 36: Exercise 2 • Pages 257–261, 300		

Welcome to *My Story K!*

Central to this study is learning to love God more and to love people more. This reflects the heart of Christ: "'And you shall love the Lord your God with all your heart, with all your soul, with all your mind, and with all your strength.' This is the first commandment. And the second, like it, is this: 'You shall love your neighbor as yourself.' There is no other commandment greater than these" (Mark 12:30–31).

The *My Story K* course is set up as follows:

- Each week, the two days of instruction are preceded by information regarding the supplies needed for that week, developmental mile markers for kindergartners, and the lesson goals of that week. Some might prefer to complete the work of both days in a single day, which is certainly possible.
- Each quarter focuses on a specific instructional area: (1) introductions to family and culture, (2) what it is to be a good citizen, (3) basic geography and understanding simple maps, and (4) basic economics and the value of things, ultimately aiming toward a better understanding of God's love for us, our families, and other people in the world.
- Faith lessons are taught concerning the value of hard work, faith/trust, kindness, peace, and more.
- Beyond the basic social studies teaching, there is a focus on appropriate language development, social and emotional development, physical development, and spiritual development for kindergartners provided for the teacher.
- During the course, the teacher will help the student develop My Book, a tear-out portion in the back of the course that is written in each week.
- Simple review times at the end of each quarter will help teachers assess learning and growth.

Developmental Mile Markers of *My Story K*

There are basic kindergarten readiness expectations for children at this age provided at the beginning of each week and based directly on the lesson topics. Though every child is created to learn and mature at his or her own pace, these markers help us be aware of what to expect. The child development focus of *My Story K* includes basic language development, social/emotional development, physical development, and spiritual development.

Developmental Mile Markers

Play: Play is such an important developmental activity for children. They can learn about cooperation, counting, taking turns, following rules, and simply having fun in life. Various games and toys can also help them learn about numbers, letters, and colors in a fun environment.

Developmental Mile Markers

Healthy Choices: You can help children make healthy choices by having them plan out simple meal ideas or think about the value of healthy foods. It is good to have children involved as much as possible with picking out healthy snacks and meals, as this helps them learn how to choose good things.

Examples

Now, let's get to the first quest!

Quest Collector Card!

QUEST ONE

Tear out this page and circle the bolded words as you find them in the lessons!

1. Strong **families** share a lot of similar things, like working together, spending time together, listening to each other, and being thankful for each other.
2. A certain area of land that is ruled by a single government and known by other countries is called a **country**.
3. The word "holiday" comes from merging the words **"holy"** and "day" because the first special days were all special religious days.
4. When we don't get enough good **foods**, we can get very sick or simply not have energy to do things.
5. **Play** is important because you can learn new words and ways to get along by playing with others.
6. Some **uniforms** are worn for special jobs, like uniforms for soldiers, or firefighters, or the police, so we can recognize those people we need when there's trouble.
7. Psalm 150 talks about giving praise to God, and it speaks of various ways we can praise Him, including using **instruments**.
8. When you are learning in books about God, or social studies, or math, remember that you should trust in **God** for your wisdom and understanding.
9. The most important book we can read is the **Bible** because it is God's Word.

GREENLAND
CANADA
USA
MEXICO
CUBA
VENEZUELA
COLOMBIA
PERU
BRAZIL
BOLIVIA
CHILE
ARGENTINA
ICELAND
UK
FRANCE
SPAIN
FINLAND
UKRAINE
TURKEY
RUSSIA
KAZAKHSTAN
MONGOLIA
CHINA
JAPAN
TAIWAN
PHILIPPINES
IRAN
IRAQ
SAUDI ARABIA
YEMEN
INDIA
MALAYSIA
INDONESIA
AUSTRALIA
NEW ZEALAND
ALGERIA
LIBYA
EGYPT
MALI
NIGER
CHAD
SUDAN
NIGERIA
SOUTH SUDAN
ETHIOPIA
SOMALIA
KENYA
CONGO
TANZANIA
ANGOLA
ZAMBIA
NAMIBIA
SOUTH AFRICA
MADAGASCAR
1
2
3
4
5
6
7
8
9
W
E
NW
NE
SW
SE
Follow the Language Time countries on the map from Lessons 1–9

On My Bike for Things I Like

My Family and Me

LESSON #1

TEACHER NOTES

Developmental Mile Markers

Basics: Though the development for young children is similar, it is so important to remember that children pass through each stage of development at their own pace. Each stage does build on the prior stage, but it is best not to try to compare children, especially with brothers and sisters in a family. Knowing what to expect from children at typical stages can help keep parents and teachers focus on the specific growth of each child.

SUPPLIES

- ☐ Crayons and Scissors
- ☐ *My Story* name tags, Scripture flashcards, Language flashcards
- ☐ Shoebox or case

Lesson Goals

Students should be able to:

- Describe how people and families are alike and different and how God loves us all.

Culture: The language, art and music, and teachings of a group of people.

A family in China

A family in India

A family in Africa

Name

Go time!

Are you ready for an adventure? Well, it's time for the first week of your first quest, and *quest* is just another word for adventure. It's go time!

Now, say this word with me: "family." How would you describe your family? Do you think your family is just like every family in the world? God actually helps us find His love in so many ways. This may come from our parents or grandparents, maybe foster families, adoptive families, or sometimes other family members who might be raising us. God is so good to be with us always and with those who take care of us.

Most people think Albert Einstein was one of the smartest people who ever lived, but not everyone thought so when he was a kid. Some people even thought he might never really learn to speak well. But once when he was sick in bed as a child, his dad brought him a compass. No matter how he moved it around, it always pointed magnetic north. He learned that there were things you couldn't see that were still very real in the world, and this sparked his interest. What sparks your interest and makes you think about wonderful things? Maybe on this quest you will learn that though we can't see God, He is very real and very much loving us every day, and His creation is all around us that shows Him to us.

Before you get too far on this quest, think about making a suitcase out of a shoebox or get a small suitcase to use for your course. Use one of your *My Story* name tags on it from the back of the book. You'll be collecting things here, including geography words and your God's Scripture Time flashcards for you to learn.

God's Scripture time

Each week for this first quest you will be learning a new verse from the Bible to try and memorize. This would be a good time to cut out your God's Scripture Time flashcards from the back of the book to put in your *My Story K* suitcase! The more we can memorize from the Bible, the more we come to know God's heart and to know how to live our lives in His love and peace. We are talking about family and **culture** in this quest, and this verse helps us know that our strength and our ability to love and help our family and others doesn't just come from us — Christ gives us the strength we need! Now listen to this verse first, then say it with me:

I can do all things through Christ who strengthens me (Philippians 4:13).

Language time!

Some people in the world speak a language called Arabic. If you want to say "thank you" in Arabic, you just say *shukran* (shoo crawn). Let's say it now, in a whisper: *shukran*. There are people in a country called Egypt who speak this language. Why don't you get your continent map of Africa from the back of the book and color in Egypt. It's also time to cut out your Language time flashcards!

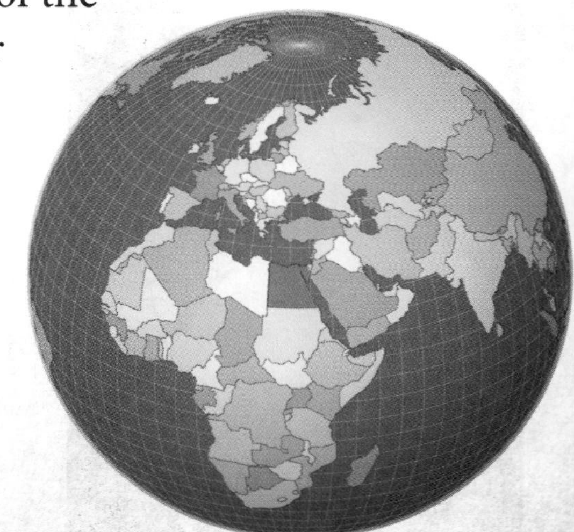

Name

MY STORY K
Lesson 1
Exercise 2 Day 2

Picture time!

This week we're talking about our families. Take some time to draw a picture of you and your family here. Think about what makes your family so special.

Helping hands time!

There are a lot of people who are part of the **culture** where you live who are wonderful helpers and heroes. Today we are going to focus on helpers and heroes right in our home! Who takes care of you? Is it your mom, or dad, or both? Or maybe you have a stepmom or stepdad, or a grandparent who cares for you. Some have other family members like aunts or uncles. Anyone in your home who cares for you and loves you is a helper and hero! Love is the light of a family. Love is shown by those who work to provide for your needs, who cook for you, who help teach you, and who keep you safe.

Talk time!

Strong families share a lot of similar things, which include helping each other, working together, spending time together, listening to each other, and being thankful for each other. Strong families also help each person meet basic needs of life, including food and shelter, health needs, emotional needs like when we are afraid or sad, and social needs. What are some of the wonderful things about your family?

My Book time!

Turn to the Lesson 1 My Book Time page in the back of this book to complete your story for the week in words and colors. Fill in the information on the top of the page, then write it into the story poem!

To Houses on Horseback
Where We Live

LESSON #2

TEACHER NOTES

Developmental Mile Markers

Self-worth: It is important to help develop a healthy sense of self-worth or self-esteem in children. For the follower of Christ, this includes the sense of worth from God's eyes, who loves us all so deeply, so wherever children live and grow up, they can know that God has placed them there for His higher purpose.

SUPPLIES

- ☐ Crayons or colored pens or pencils

Lesson Goals

Students should be able to:

- Identify the different kinds of places where people live; identify the city and country where they live; and know what a neighborhood is, as well as a city, state/province, and country.

Country: A certain area of land ruled by a single government and known by other countries.

Children waving the flag in Dubai

A girl waves the flag of Israel

A girl waves the flag of the United States on Independence Day

Name

Go time! A new week is beginning. Come on, it's go time!

Where do people live on the earth? Everywhere! Some live in cities or towns with lots of houses, business places, and parks. Some live in the countryside with lots of open land and fewer people. Living in a city is very different from living in a town, but both are great places to live!

If you don't already know, ask your teacher what city you live in or near. Then find out what state, province, or territory you live in. And then what **country** you live in! You can ask your teacher to help you find your **country** on a map or globe.

Also, the people of God's world speak over 7,000 languages. And while English has 26 letters that you may already know, if you were writing in Chinese, there are around 5,000 characters. The language you speak often depends on where you live. What language do you speak? Do you speak more than one language?

Now, let's see if we can learn a little something about countries, governments, and flags.

- What is a **country**? A **country** is a certain area of land ruled by a single government and known by other countries.
- What is a government? A government is made up of people who make laws that each person in the **country** must follow. Some countries pick their leaders, and this is generally called a democracy. Some countries have kings or queens, and this is called a monarchy. And there are other types of governments too.
- Why are there flags for the various countries? Flags are symbols of a state, a province or territory, or a **country**. Each picture, word, and color mean something for the people the flag represents.

Ask your teacher what kind of government your country has. Do you know what your country's flag looks like? Find a picture of it and color it here!

God's Scripture time

Get your God's Scripture Time flashcards ready! We are talking about where we live in this lesson, and in this verse, we hear God tell us that He is with us no matter where we are, so we don't need to worry! Now listen to this verse first, then say it with me:

Fear not, for I am with you . . . (Isaiah 43:5).

Language 07:00 time!

Some people in the world speak a language called Armenian. If you want to say "thank you" in Armenian, you just say *shnorhagallem* (snore hey gallem). Let's say it now, in a calm way: *shnorhagallem*. There are people in a **country** called Armenia who speak this language. Why don't you get your continent map of Asia and color in Armenia!

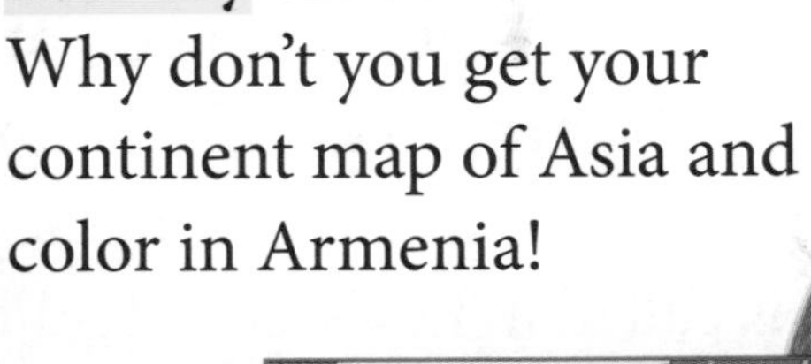

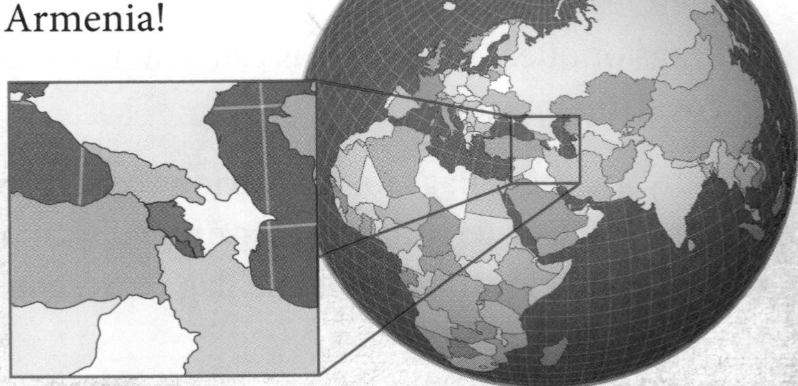

Name

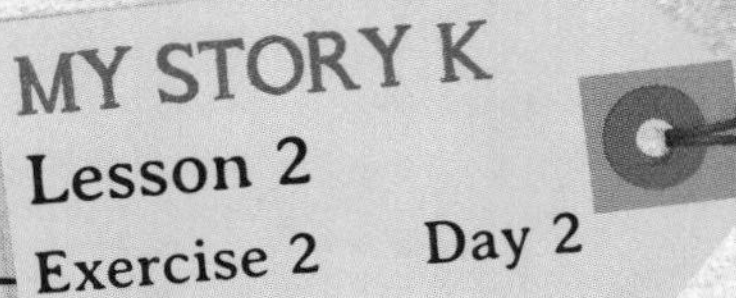

Picture time! Look at the pictures and circle the one that best shows what your home is like.

How would you describe your home? Do you know what it is made out of? Well, around the world, homes are sometimes made from wood, cement, stone, mud, bricks, branches, animal skins, metal, cardboard boxes, and more. But more than that, homes are places we should feel safe and loved — places where God gives us peace in His presence.

Trace over the path with a pencil or crayon to help the bird, bee, and fox find their way home.

There are many people who help make our communities better places. A community is a group of people who live and work close together. Some in your community are builders who help create and build the homes we live in. Some design the homes by creating what is called a blueprint. These are the architects. Some take these drawings and begin to build the homes, and these include the ones who lay concrete for foundations, build the frame of the houses, and lay brick or stone for the outside of the house. There are also electricians who put wires in the house for electricity, plumbers who put in the pipes, roofers, cabinet workers, carpet and flooring workers, and so many others. Let's take a moment to thank God for all these people who make our homes for us so we can find shelter from the storms, from the cold, and from the heat!

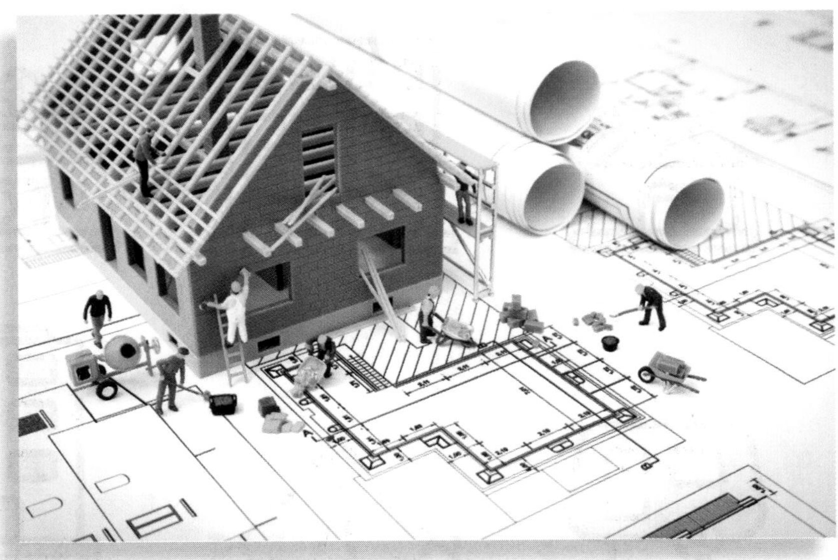

Where you grow up often helps shape who you are when you grow up. Each community is just a little different than all the others. So, what is your community like? And your home? How does it make you feel? Why is it special to you?

Turn to the Lesson 2 My Book Time page in the back of this book to complete your story for the week in words and colors!

Scooters to Celebrations

Holidays and Special Times

LESSON #3

TEACHER NOTES

Developmental Mile Markers

Healthy Emotions: You can help children develop healthy emotional responses by talking with them about their emotions, letting them know that emotions are natural, and teaching them ways to cope with anger or sorrow. This can be especially true at holidays and special times for kids who do best with routine. Talk out how a particular day or week will be different and how they can be ready for this experience.

SUPPLIES

- ☐ Crayons or colored pens or pencils

Lesson Goals

Students should be able to:

- Describe some of the holidays celebrated around the world and know that people everywhere have special days that help them appreciate their world more.

A family watching fireworks on New Years Eve

Holiday: A special day to celebrate, made from the words "holy" and "day."

Nativity scene reenactment

A Thanksgiving feast

Palm Sunday in East Timor

Name

MY STORY K
Lesson 3
Exercise 1 Day 1

Go time!

A new week is here to learn and grow. Come on, it's go time!

Family enjoying celebration at home

This week we are talking about holidays and special days, specifically autumn days. We usually think of a **holiday** as a time we get to have off to spend with our family and friends. The word ***holiday*** comes from merging the words "holy" and "day" because the first special days were all special religious days.

Now, a **holiday** might include special celebration times for the community or country. So, if you are in Vietnam in the fall, you might celebrate the Children's Festival, which is celebrated with the harvest in October. If you live in Canada, you might celebrate Thanksgiving in October — while in the United States, it is celebrated in November — giving thanks to God for the harvest and all the good He has done. On November 14th in India, you might celebrate Children's Day, which views children as the strength and hope of the nation.

A family video calling on Thanksgiving

In the Bible, there are many holy days mentioned. This includes the Sabbath (Exodus 20:11), Rosh Hashanah or Feast of Trumpets (Leviticus 23:22–25), Yom Kippur or the Day of Atonement (Leviticus 23:26–32), and Passover (Leviticus 23:4–5). You can read more about them in God's Word!

Get your God's Scripture Time flashcards ready! We are talking about holidays and special times in this lesson, and in this verse we are told to be kind and forgiving to one another just like God is kind and forgiving to us! So, whether you're celebrating a Saturday off or celebrating Jesus' birthday, remember to be kind always. Now listen to this verse first, then say it with me:

> *And be kind to one another, tenderhearted, forgiving one another, even as God in Christ forgave you* (Philippians 4:13).

Language 07:00 time!

Some people in the world speak a language called Bosnian. If you want to say "thank you" in Bosnian, you just say *hvala* (hvah lah). Let's say it now, in a slow way: *hvala*. There are people in a country called Bosnia who speak this language. Why don't you get your continent map of Europe and color in Bosnia!

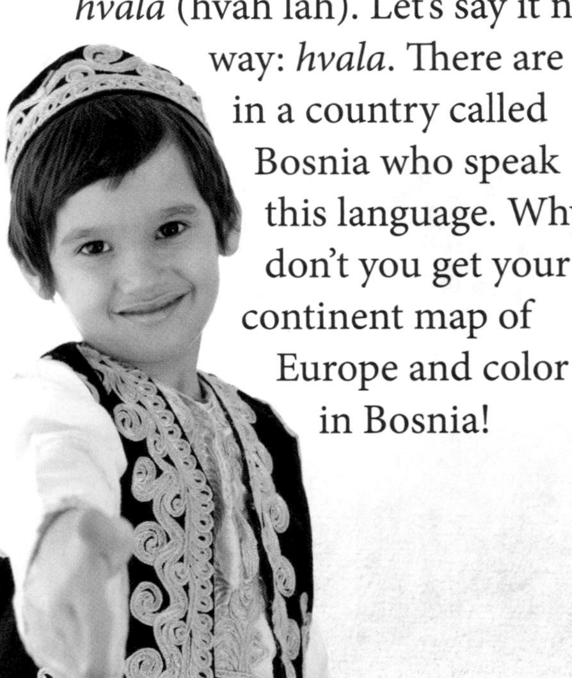

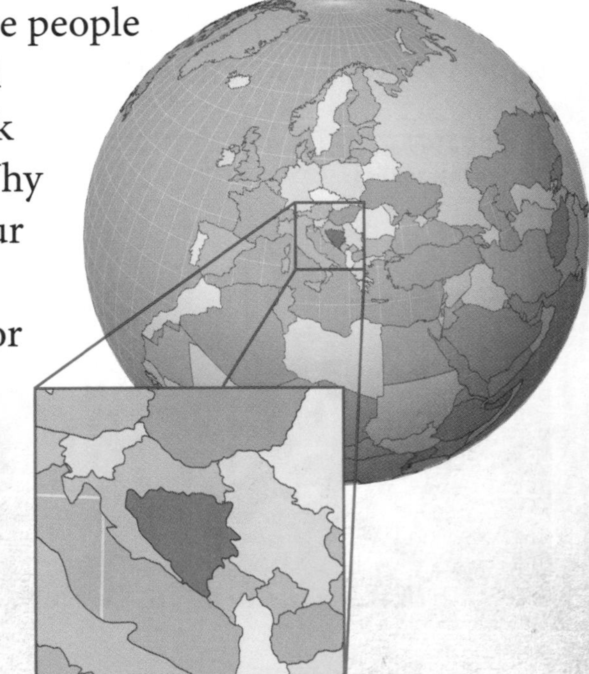

Name

MY STORY K
Lesson 3
Exercise 2 Day 2

Picture time! Color this picture of a birthday celebration.

Helping hands time!

Because so many in our communities celebrate special events, including birthdays and **holiday** times, there are lots of people who help provide special things for us to celebrate with. These helpers make sure we have everything we need so our events are happy and blessed, including party store workers who supply balloons and other supplies, party planners who help coordinate fun events, bakers who make us delicious cakes and other desserts, and park workers who keep city parks clean and beautiful.

We all have days that are special to us, make us happy, or make us feel peaceful. What is a favorite special day that you look forward to in the year? Why is it special to you?

Turn to the Lesson 3 My Book Time page in the back of this book to complete your story for the week in words and colors!

On Roller Skates with Delicious Plates

Good Food and Nutrition

LESSON #4

TEACHER NOTES

Developmental Mile Markers

Healthy Choices: You can help children make healthy choices by having them plan out simple meal ideas or think about the value of healthy foods. It is good to have children involved as much as possible with picking out healthy snacks and meals, as this helps them learn how to choose good things.

Lesson Goals

Students should be able to:

- Understand how important good nutrition is and that we can help others be strong and healthy too.

SUPPLIES

- ☐ Crayons or colored pens or pencils

Nutrition: The act of eating good food and drinks to keep you healthy.

Name

MY STORY K
Lesson 4
Exercise 1 Day 1

Go time!

Roller skates? Delicious plates? Yes, because it's go time!

Food seems very basic, but it is so important for us to live. It is the fuel that gives us strength and energy. All of us! When we don't get enough good foods, we can get very sick or simply not have energy to do things. That's why we need to study good **nutrition**. Sadly, about 15 percent of the world goes to bed hungry.

Sharing food together at mealtime is the perfect way to spend time with your family. In the Bible, people would break bread together. This meant sharing a meal, as well as talking, laughing, and praying with each other. These special times help us get closer as a family.

There are many ways to prepare food for meals, whether cooking over a fire, in an oven, or in a microwave. In some parts of the world, people use up to 80 percent of their money on food to live. That means that they use $8 out of every $10 they have for things like rice, bread, fruits, and vegetables. In places like the United States, it is usually about 10 percent of the income, or $1 out of every $10.

Rice is definitely one of the foods that helps keep billions of people alive each day. Grains of rice are a type of grass seed that grow in very wet places. What are some of your favorite foods?

God's Scripture time

Get your God's Scripture Time flashcards ready! We are talking about good food and nutrition in this lesson, and in this verse we are giving God praise because He made us so wonderfully! He knows what we need to eat and drink to help us stay strong. Now listen to this verse first, then say it with me:

I will praise You, for I am fearfully and wonderfully made; Marvelous are Your works, And that my soul knows very well (Psalm 139:14).

Language 07:00 time!

Some people in the world speak a language called Bulgarian. If you want to say "thank you" in Bulgarian, you just say *blagodaria* (blah guh darria). Let's say it now, in a brave way: *blagodaria*. There are people in a country called Bulgaria who speak this language. Why don't you get your continent map of Europe and color in Bulgaria!

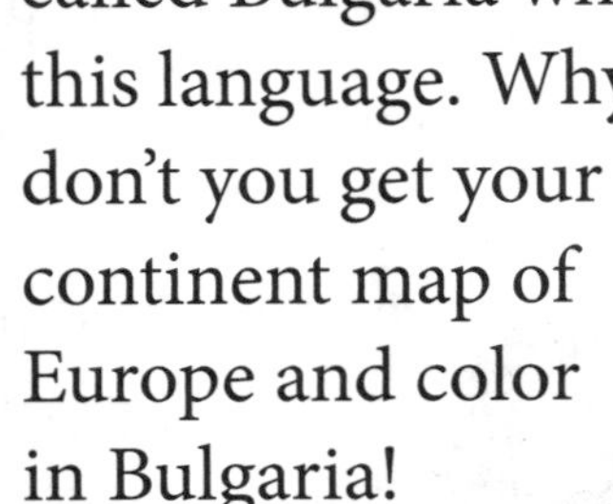

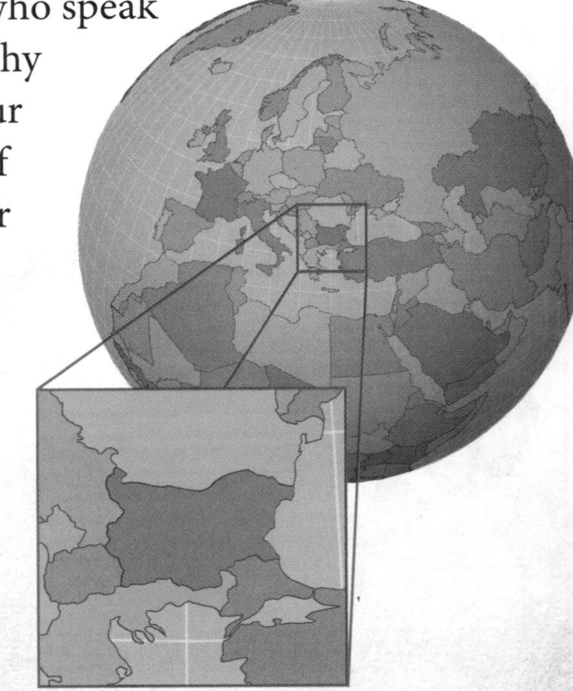

Name ______________________________

Picture time!

Color this bowl of delicious fruit.

Helping hands time!

Did you know there are people in our communities who try to make sure that others stay healthy and well fed? That's right! Some are called nutritionists, who teach about eating good foods that keep your body strong. There are also farmers who grow healthy fruits and vegetables and sell them at farmer's markets or stores. Others include grocery workers who sell good food, chefs and restaurant workers who serve prepared food to people, and beekeepers who care for bees and help gather their honey for us to eat.

Talk time!

Eating good food is very important, especially when you're young and still growing. Your body and brain need the best **nutrition** to grow strong and healthy. What would you say are the three healthiest things you eat or drink each week? Why is eating a healthy diet so important?

My Book time!

Turn to the Lesson 4 My Book Time page in the back of this book to complete your story for the week in words and colors!

Skateboard Day and Things We Play

Games and Toys

LESSON #5

TEACHER NOTES

Developmental Mile Markers

Play: Play is such an important developmental activity for children. They can learn about cooperation, counting, taking turns, following rules, and simply having fun in life. Various games and toys can also help them learn about numbers, letters, and colors in a fun environment.

SUPPLIES

- ☐ Crayons or colored pens or pencils
- ☐ Scissors
- ☐ Tape

Lesson Goals

Students should be able to:

- Describe various games and toys from around the world and how play can actually help us learn.

Play: Activity that is fun and can help us learn as well.

Name

Go time!

Our skateboards are going to take us through the new week. Here it is, it's go time!

A long time ago (in 1560), a man named Pieter Bruegel painted a picture that he called *Children's Games*. It shows over 80 different games that children used to **play** at that time. You can see children rolling hoops, shooting marbles, playing with dolls, playing leapfrog, wearing costume masks, having a tug of war, and so much more. Look below and see how many games you can find!

Some people think of playing as just wasting time, but **play** is very important, especially for kids! You can learn certain physical skills by balancing or running. You can learn certain thinking skills like math when playing store. You can learn new words and ways to get along by playing with others. Even just coloring can help you learn to write for when you're older.

Get your God's Scripture Time flashcards ready! We are talking about games and toys in this lesson, and in this verse we learn that we should be rejoicing or filled with joy in the Lord always! He is so good to us, and as we **play** we can find extra joy in praising the Lord for blessings in our life. Now listen to this verse first, then say it with me:

Rejoice in the Lord always. Again I will say, rejoice! (Philippians 4:4).

Language 07:00 time!

Some people in the world speak a language called Bengali. If you want to say "thank you" in Bengali, you just say *dhanyabad* (doon yaw bawd). Let's say it now, in a singing way: *dhanyabad*. There are people in a country called Bangladesh who speak this language. Why don't you get your continent map of Asia and color in Bangladesh!

Name

Have your teacher help you cut out and tape the toy car together, like the sample one pictured here!

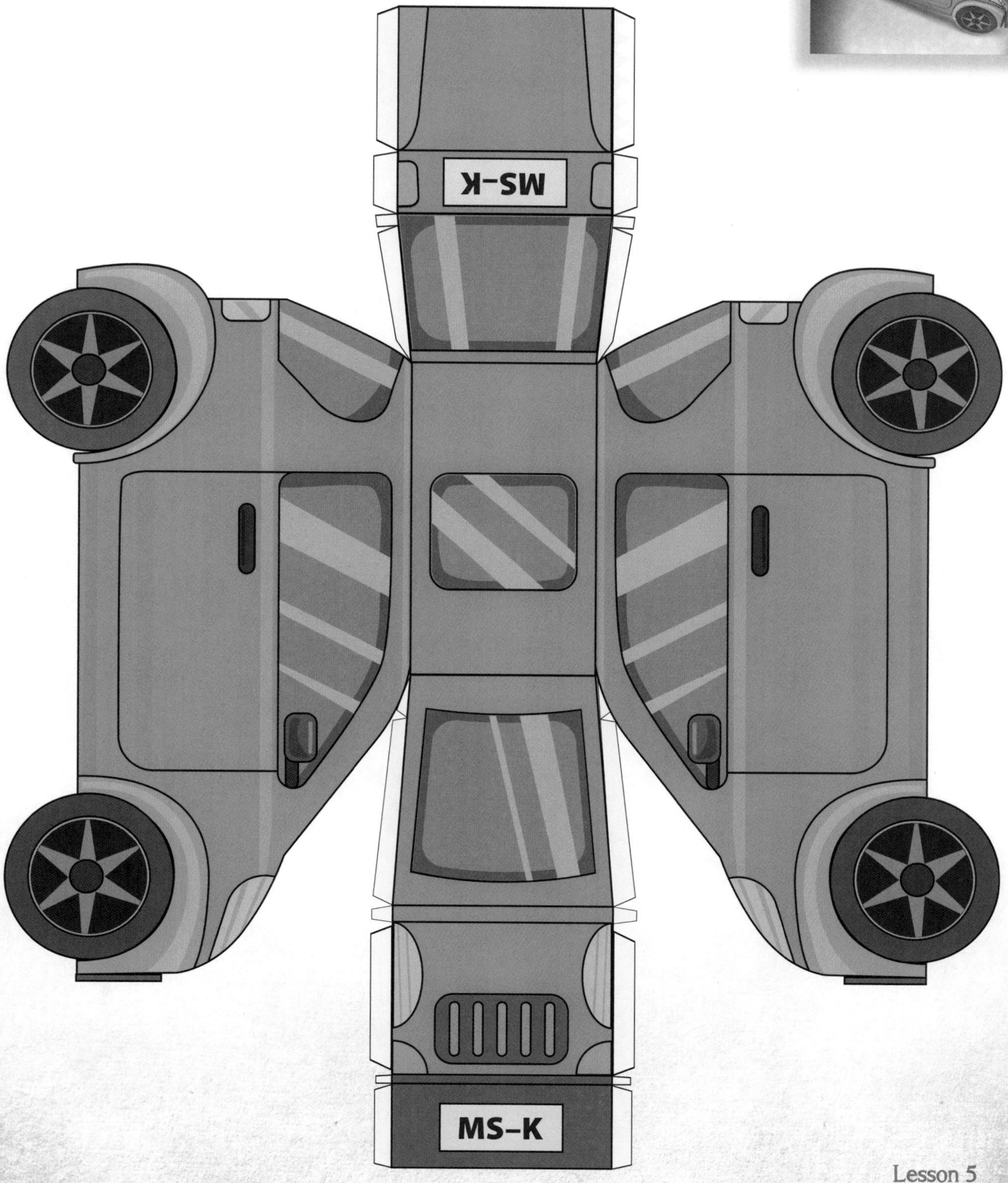

MS–K

MS–K

Page blank for cutting purposes.

Helping hands time!

There have been games and toys for kids to **play** with for thousands of years! However, most of the really old ones were handmade by families or friends. More recently, companies have been making fun things for kids and their families. These are the game and toy makers in our communities. And how do you get those fun creations after they are made in a factory? Why, often postal workers bring them to special toy store workers who display them or bring them directly to you!

Play is something that helps you grow in many ways, and that means playing indoors or outdoors! What are your favorite games to **play** outside? What about inside games?

Turn to the Lesson 5 My Book Time page in the back of this book to complete your story for the week in words and colors!

Snow Sleds and Colorful Threads

Clothing and Uniforms

LESSON #6

TEACHER NOTES

Developmental Mile Markers

Fine Motor Skills: Children 4 to 5 years old should be able to write out some of their letters and button their clothing. Find jackets or costumes that make it fun for them to practice their buttoning skills.

Lesson Goals

Students should be able to:

- Recognize various uniforms that first responders and others wear, as well as special clothing that different groups wear to highlight their culture and history.

SUPPLIES

- ☐ Crayons or colored pens or pencils

word collector **Uniform**: A kind of costume worn by people in a special group, like nurses or the police.

Go time!

It feels so cold, it must be time for snow sleds! Get ready because it's go time!

Look at the many different kinds of clothing worn by people around the world. So many styles and so many colors! Some of these different types of clothing represent the history of a people group or a country. Some are festive outfits for special holidays. And some will wear a **uniform** for special jobs, like a **uniform** for a medical worker, firefighter, or the police, so we can recognize those people we need when there's trouble. It's good to get to know people in your neighborhood or community who can assist you and your family when you need help.

Couple dressed in costume of past Europe

It takes years to become a geisha

Newlyweds in India wearing traditional wedding clothing

God's Scripture time

Get your God's Scripture Time flashcards ready! We are talking about clothing and uniforms in this lesson, and in this verse, we learn that one of the most important things we can do is love our neighbors as much as we love ourselves. So, no matter what outfit or **uniform** our neighbor wears, we need to find ways to love them, even if it's only sharing a smile and a wave. Now listen to this verse first, then say it with me:

You shall love your neighbor as yourself (Matthew 22:39).

Language time!

Some people in the world speak a language called Cherokee. If you want to say "thank you" in Cherokee, you just say *wado* (waw doe). Let's say it now, quietly: *wado*. There are people in a country called the United States who speak this language. Why don't you get your continent map of North America and color in the United States (all except for Hawaii)!

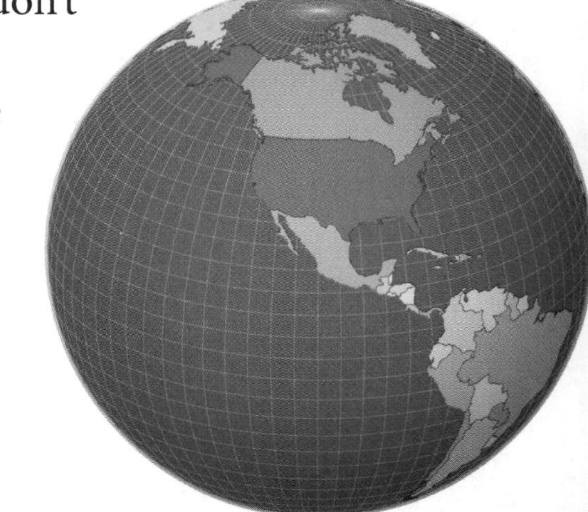

Name

Picture time!

Color the following hats. Can you tell which hat belongs to a policeman? A soldier? A ship captain? A graduate? A sheriff? A pirate?

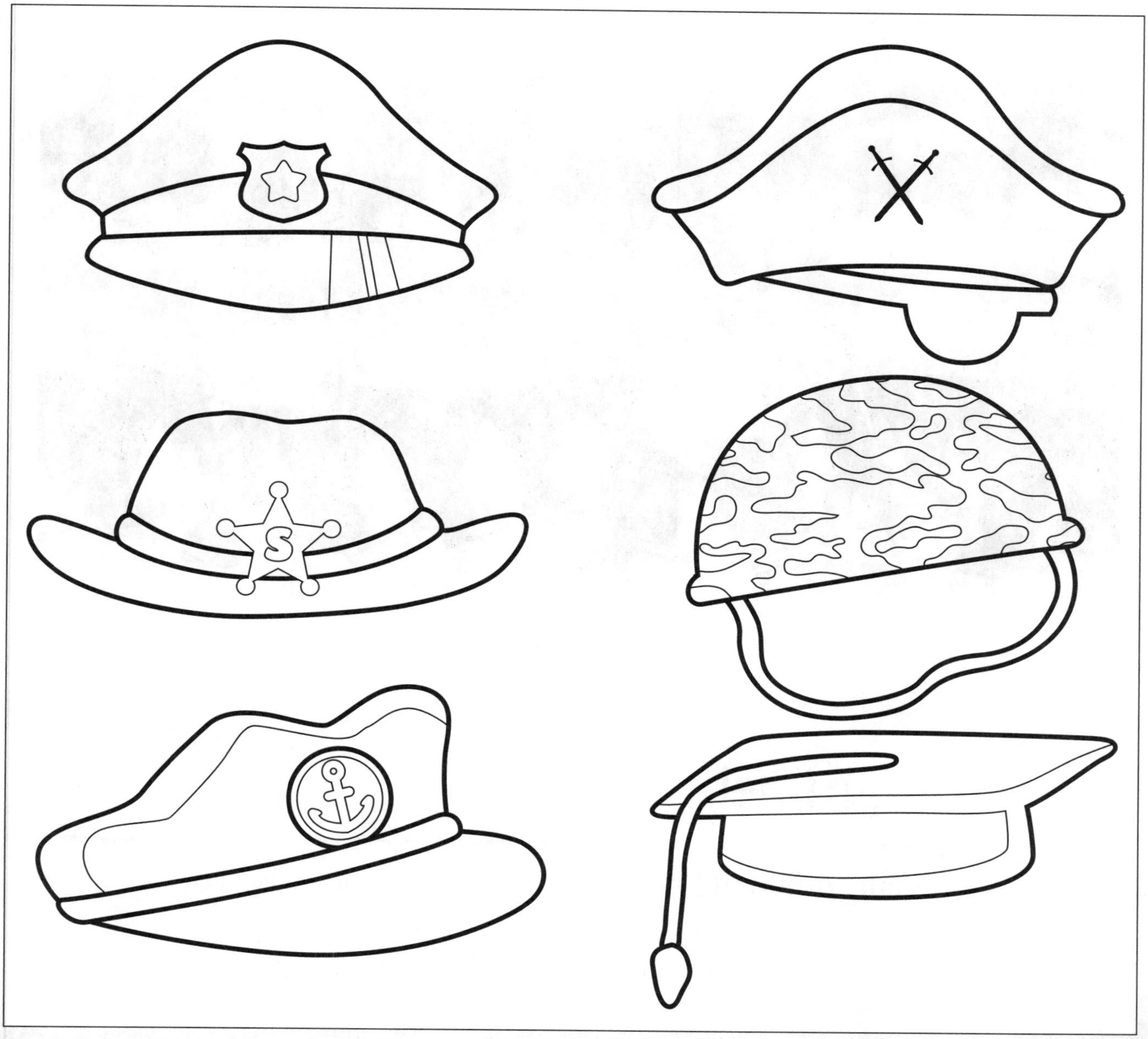

Helping hands time!

Have you ever been to a parade or watched one on television? Often you get to see people in **uniform** marching down the street. Some of these people help watch over us to keep us safe, and these helpers include the police, the ones who keep the peace in our communities; firefighters, the ones who protect us when fires get out of control; and ambulance drivers, the ones who help us get safely to the hospital when we're injured. Some play instruments and march together as a band!

Talk time!

There are so many different kinds of uniforms that people wear for their work! Each one has a different purpose and a different style. Why do you think there are so many kinds of uniforms? Which **uniform** would you like to wear if you could?

My Book time!

Turn to the Lesson 6 My Book Time page in the back of this book to complete your story for the week in words and colors!

In My Wheelchair with Music in the Air

Music and Song

LESSON #7

TEACHER NOTES

Developmental Mile Markers

Play: Individual play helps children expand their imaginations. Playing with others can help develop a sense of teamwork. This play can involve music and songs, which have long been known to help with memory skills.

Lesson Goals

Students should be able to:

- Identify various kinds of instruments that people play and know that instruments can be used to praise and honor God.

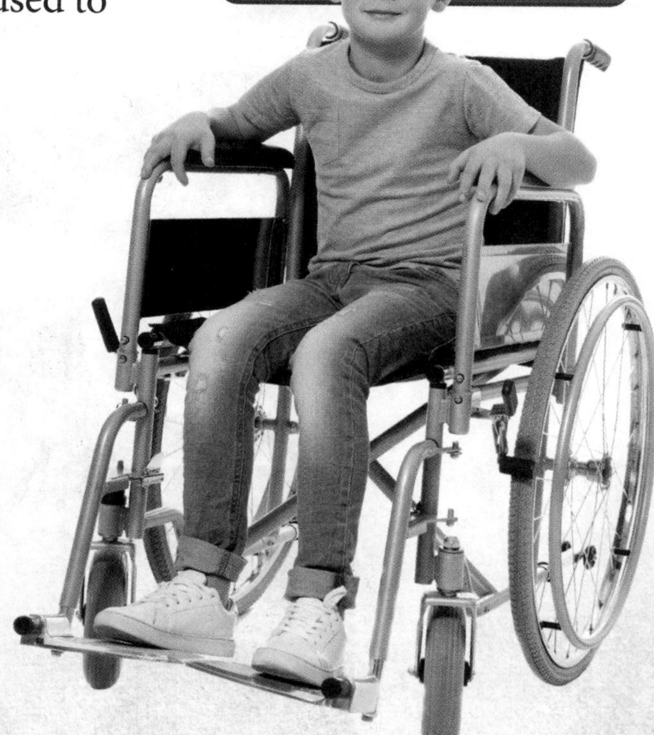

word collector **Psalm**: A special song that gives praise to God.

Name

MY STORY K
Lesson 7
Exercise 1 Day 1

God's given us a new week to share. Come along, it's go time!

In the Bible, there is a book called Psalms. A **psalm** is a sacred song, and the psalms in the Bible give praise and honor to God for His goodness and for His might. **Psalm** 150 talks about giving praise to God, speaking of the various ways we can praise Him, including using instruments:

Praise the LORD!
Praise God in His sanctuary;
Praise Him in His mighty firmament!
Praise Him for His mighty acts;
Praise Him according to His excellent greatness!
Praise Him with the sound of the trumpet;
Praise Him with the lute and harp!
Praise Him with the timbrel and dance;
Praise Him with stringed instruments and flutes!
Praise Him with loud cymbals;
Praise Him with clashing cymbals!
Let everything that has breath praise the LORD.
Praise the LORD!

Do you recognize some of the instruments mentioned in the psalm? Using instruments for praise is such a wonderful way to show God we love Him!

God's Scripture time

Get your God's Scripture Time flashcards ready! We are talking about music and song in this lesson, and in this verse, we learn that when we keep God's commandments, we learn of love. And just like in a song where there is a harmony and a melody, love for God and others brings a beautiful music to the world. Now listen to this verse first, then say it with me:

For this is the love of God, that we keep His commandments. And His commandments are not burdensome (1 John 5:3).

Language time!

Some people in the world speak a language called Croatian. If you want to say "thank you" in Croatian, you just say *hvala* (hvah lah). Let's say it now, loudly: *hvala*. There are people in a country called Croatia who speak this language. Why don't you get your continent map of Europe and color in Croatia!

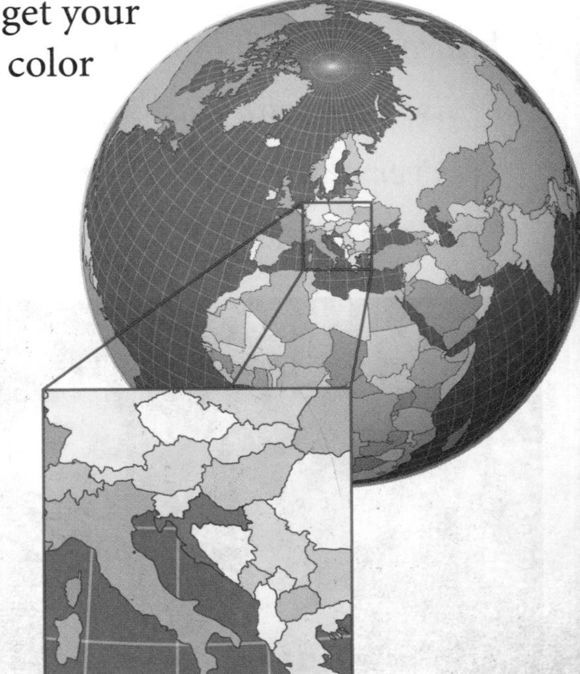

Name

Picture time!

It is so wonderful to learn to play instruments. Color this page and see if you can name some of the instruments these children are playing. Can you find someone playing the piano, a drum, a trumpet, a guitar, a violin, a flute, and an accordion? Do you play an instrument, or would you like to learn one? What is your favorite instrument to listen to?

Helping hands time!

If you really like music, you might grow up to work in a music career one day. These are the people in our communities who either teach us about music or who play music to entertain or inspire us. Some churches have musicians who help lead us in worship with their voices or with instruments. Some in our communities are pianists, violinists, or drummers who lift us with their songs, while some are singers who lift us with their voices. And all of these can be a part of musical theater that tells stories through song.

Talk time!

Music is filled with lots of emotion, just like a **psalm** in the Bible. It can make you feel happy, or sad, or excited, or worshipful toward God. Do you like listening to music? What is your favorite kind of music or your favorite song?

My Book time!

Turn to the Lesson 7 My Book Time page in the back of this book to complete your story for the week in words and colors!

On a Trike with Books I Like

Pictures and Words in Books

LESSON #8

TEACHER NOTES

Developmental Mile Markers

The Joy of Reading Out Loud: One of the most educationally inspiring things a parent can do is to read to his or her child. The joy of reading is most often a skill caught by young children as someone reads to them, letting them experience the happiness of hearing a story spoken to them, something even some young readers still love. Remember to find books you love to read, to make this reading time feel special, to show the children the pictures as you read, to have them learn about people around the world, and to have this special time every day.

Lesson Goals

Students should be able to:

- Recognize certain basic words as they begin building their vocabulary through seeing words and hearing them spoken.

word collector **Words**: Letters or sounds that mean something to people.

Name

We have so much more to learn. Come on, it's go time!

Did you know that there are many children in the world who are not taught to read or write? And these children grow up to be adults who don't know how to read or write. Can you imagine not being able to enjoy a good book? But getting an education is more than just learning to read; it gives people a sense of joy in who they are.

There are so many good books in the world filled with **words** and pictures. You might already be learning your letters. If so, can you recognize the letters below? Letters are connected together to make **words**. And sometimes, rather than using letters and **words**, we use pictures because they can teach us too.

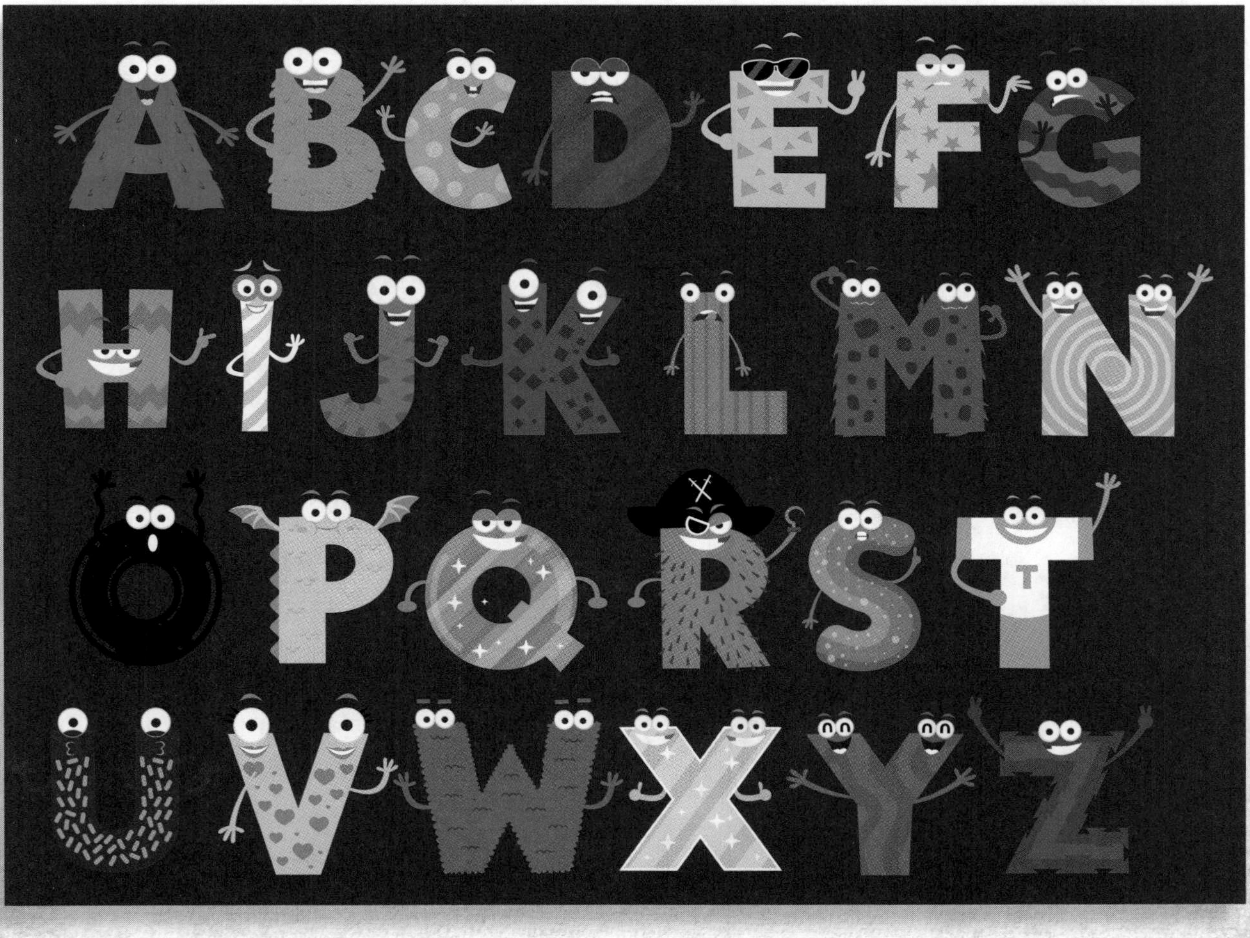

God's Scripture time

Get your God's Scripture Time flashcards ready! We are talking about pictures and **words** in books in this lesson. In this week's verse, we learn that we should trust in the Lord completely. So, when you are learning in books about God, or social studies, or math, remember that you should trust in God for your wisdom and understanding. Now listen to this verse first, then say it with me:

Trust in the L*ORD* *with all your heart, and lean not on your own understanding* (Proverbs 3:5).

Language time!

Some people in the world speak a language called Czech. If you want to say "thank you" in Czech, you just say *dekuji* (dye koo yih). Let's say it now, bravely: *dekuji*. There are people in a country called the Czech Republic who speak this language. Why don't you get your continent map of Europe and color in the Czech Republic!

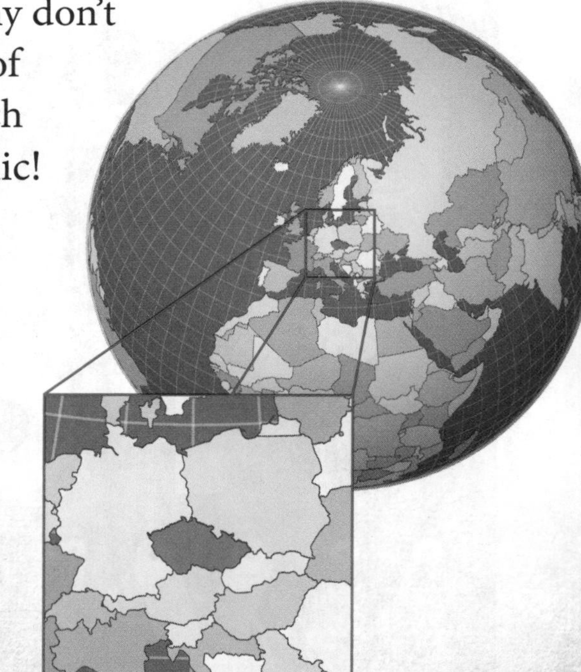

Name ______________________________

Picture time!

Match the word on the left with the image it goes with on the right by drawing a line between them.

food 

drink 

happy 

sad 

Every community has people in it who love books and who make a living sharing their love of books. It can be wonderful to see the story of how a book gets into your hands! Books start as **words** in the mind and heart of an author who writes or types them down. Then editors help them make sure the **words** are just right, artists make pictures based on the **words**, and designers at publishing companies create the look of a book in a special way with the pictures and **words** all together. This book file is then sent to a printer to make the actual book on paper, which is sent to homes and libraries across the country. Now it's your turn to enjoy the book!

Books can teach us about the world or can take us on journeys around the world. What do you like best about books? Do you have a favorite book you look at or have someone read to you?

Turn to the Lesson 8 My Book Time page in the back of this book to complete your story for the week in **words** and colors!

Zipline and Language Time

Reading and Writing

TEACHER NOTES

End of week recipe ingredients:

- ☐ 2 cups all-purpose flour
- ☐ 1¼ cups plain yogurt (Greek or regular)
- ☐ 2 teaspoons baking powder
- ☐ ¼ teaspoon salt

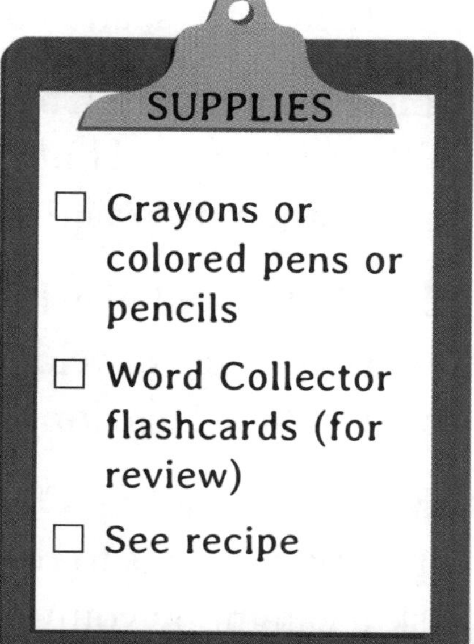

Developmental Mile Markers Review

Basics: Though the development for young children is similar, it is so important to remember that children pass through each stage of development at their own pace. Each stage does build on the prior stage, but it is best not to try to compare children, especially with brothers and sisters in a family. Knowing what to expect from children at typical stages can help keep parents and teachers focused on the specific growth of each child.

Self-worth: It is important to help develop a healthy sense of self-worth or self-esteem in children. For the follower of Christ, this includes the sense of worth from God's eyes, who loves us all so deeply. So wherever children live and grow up, they can know that God has placed them there for His higher purpose.

Healthy Emotions: You can help children develop healthy emotional responses by talking with them about their emotions, letting them know that emotions are natural, and teaching them ways to cope with anger or sorrow. This can be especially true at holidays and special times for kids who do best with routine. Talk out how a particular day or week will be different and how they can be ready for this experience.

Healthy Choices: You can help children make healthy choices by having them plan out simple meal ideas or think about the value of healthy foods. It is good to have children involved as much as possible with picking out healthy snacks and meals, as this helps them learn how to choose good things.

Play: Play is such an important developmental activity for children. They can learn about cooperation, counting, taking turns, following rules, and simply having fun in life. Various games and toys can also help them learn about numbers, letters, and colors in a fun environment.

Fine Motor Skills: Children 4 to 5 years old should be able to write out some of their letters and button their clothing. Find jackets or costumes that make it fun for them to practice their buttoning skills.

Play: Individual play helps children expand their imaginations. Playing with others can help develop a sense of teamwork. This play can involve music and songs, which have long been known to help with memory skills.

The Joy of Reading Out Loud: One of the most educationally inspiring things a parent can do is to read to his or her child. The joy of reading is most often a skill caught by young children as someone reads to them, letting them experience the happiness of hearing a story spoken to them, something even some young readers still love. Remember to find books you love to read, to make this reading time feel special, to show the children the pictures as you read, to have them learn about people around the world, and to have this special time every day.

Lesson Goals

Students should be able to:

- Describe a little of the history of words, first depicted as pictures and then represented by connecting letters to form words.

Symbols: A picture that means something to people.

Name ___________________________________

Go time!

The last week of your first quest? Yes, it's go time!

Long ago in a place called Egypt, they used something called hieroglyphs to write about their world. These were pictures or **symbols** that meant something to the people long ago. Now many people use emojis to tell about emotions and more. These are pictures that people send each other to say "I love you" or "I'm happy." Emojis were first created by a man named Shigetaka Kurita. What is important to learn when you are first beginning to read and write is that letters (like A and D) and words (like "hello") are also **symbols**.

Learning to read involves figuring out **symbols**. These would be the **symbols** for letters that combine to make words, as well as **symbols** for words themselves. But what is most is important is being able to understand the words we read or that someone reads to us. You might be able to figure out how a word sounds by looking at it, but understanding what it means can take a long time. This is why it is so important for you to have people who read to you. See if you can save even 15 or 20 minutes a day to have reading time. You might say back what was read to you and ask questions if you have any. Reading can be fun, and we can learn so much about the world from a book. Also, reading the Bible helps us understand God's love for us and how we can love others more!

God's Scripture time

Get your God's Scripture Time flashcards ready! We are talking about reading and writing in this lesson. In this week's verse, we learn that we should believe on the name of Jesus and love each other. The most important book we can read is the Bible because it is God's Word. When we read it, we learn His heart for us and for our world. Now listen to this verse first, then say it with me:

And this is His commandment: that we should believe on the name of His Son Jesus Christ and love one another, as He gave us commandment (1 John 3:23).

Language time!

Some people in the world speak a language called Dutch. If you want to say "thank you" in Dutch, you just say *dank u* (dawn koo). Let's say it now, in a whisper: *dank u*. There are people in a country called Curaçao who speak this language. Why don't you get your continent map of South America and color in Curaçao!

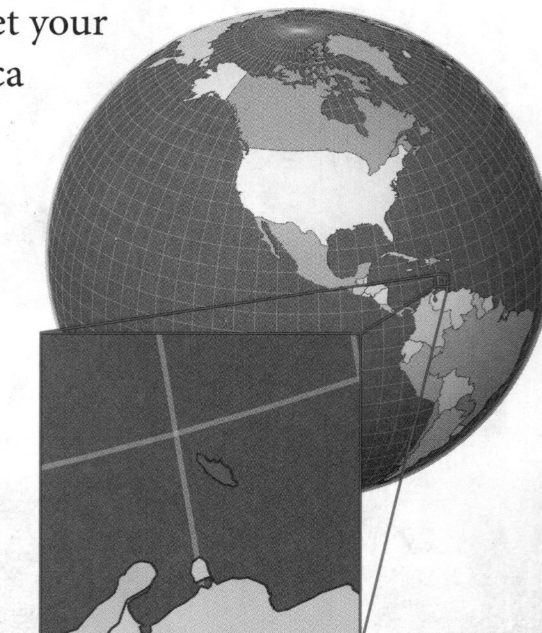

Traditional Dutch clothing from Holland

Name

Picture time!

DOT-TO-DOT: Complete the dot-to-dot starting with **a**, the first letter of the alphabet, and finishing at **z**, the last letter of the alphabet. Then color.

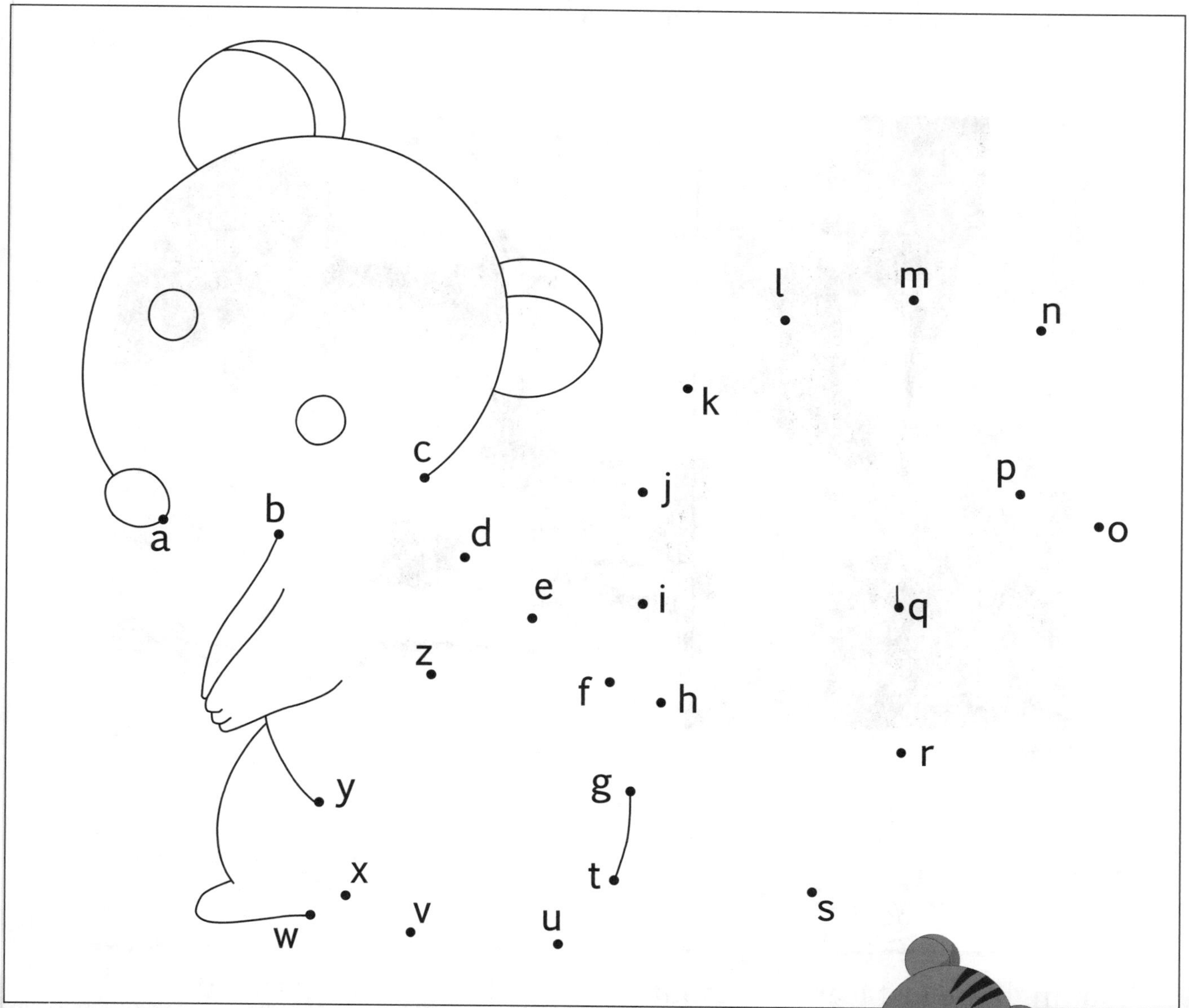

a b c d e f g h i j k l m n o p q r s t u v w x y z

Now is a special time when you are just learning to start reading and writing letters, numbers, and **symbols**. Everyone grows at a different pace and with different skills and gifts because that's how God created us! Know that in every community there are people who help us learn reading and writing skills, including parents and caregivers who are often our teachers. Also, there are speech therapists who can help us speak more clearly, eye doctors who can help us see what we are reading more clearly, and bookstores and libraries that provide books for us as we learn the joy of reading.

You might be just learning about reading and writing in this school year. If you were able to write a book, what kind of book would you like to create?

Turn to the Lesson 9 My Book Time page in the back of this book to complete your story for the week in words and colors!

Food Time

Breads Around the World!

At the end of each quest, we will be looking at the different types of foods people around the world eat. More specifically, we will be learning about staples. Staples are food items that we eat every day, sometimes at every meal.

The first staple we'll be looking at is bread. What each different type of bread looks like and its ingredients may be different, but throughout the world, there is some type of bread at our tables.

Go to your pantry, bread box, or refrigerator, wherever you keep bread. What types of bread do you have in your house? When do you eat bread? Do you have toast for breakfast? A sandwich for lunch? Do you have bread at dinner?

Look at the map from around the world. How many different kinds of bread have you tried before?

Here's a recipe to try and make with your teacher:

Naan

India,
the Middle East,
and throughout
Asia

Ingredients

☐ 2 cups all-purpose flour or gluten-free baking flour

☐ 1¼ cups plain yogurt (Greek or regular)

☐ 2 teaspoons baking powder

☐ ¼ teaspoon salt

Place all four ingredients together in a large bowl. Use your hands to form the dough into a ball while still in the bowl. Knead the dough for about a minute. It will be slightly sticky. Add flour to the dough if needed to make it easier to handle.

Divide it into six equal pieces. Dust a rolling pin with flour and roll each ball into a 6" to 8" circle. It may be slightly oval, and that is fine too.

Teacher should heat a frying pan (cast iron is best) until hot. No oil is needed. Cook for 1–2 minutes on each side until bread begins to puff up a bit and is slightly blistered or toasted in spots.

Naan is best served warm. It can be brushed with butter or olive oil.

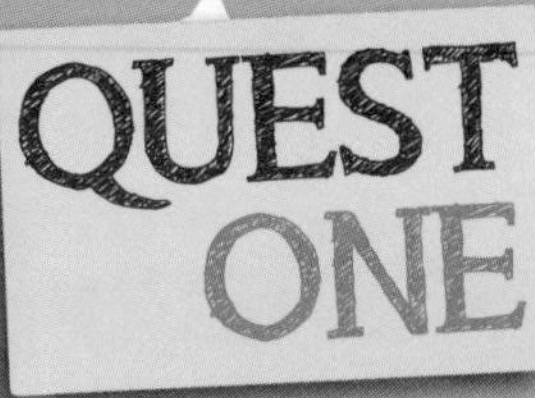

CONGRATULATIONS!

____

Name

Finished Quest One of *My Story K!*

____

Date

Quest Collector Card!

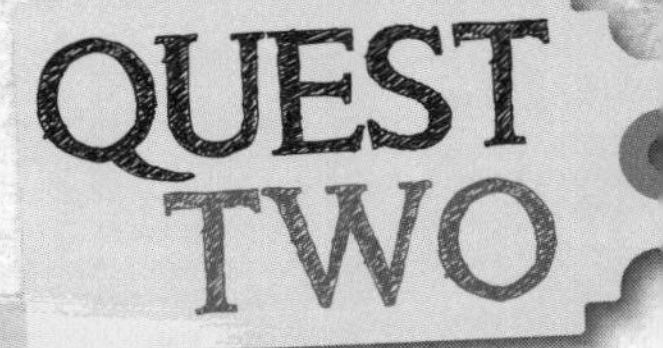

Tear out this page and circle the bolded words as you find them in the lessons!

1. Philippians 4:13 says that "I can do **all** things through Christ who strengthens me."
2. Laws are created for many reasons, but one main reason is to keep people **safe** from harm.
3. We don't need to be afraid of things because **God** is watching over us.
4. Traditions or **customs** are events that are believed and followed over the course of time.
5. The best **friends** are those who pray with us and for us, who are patient and kind, and who make us feel God's joy in the time we share with them.
6. When we honor God by loving others as He wants us to, we will find ways of bringing **peace** at times when family or friends might be fighting.
7. Many who serve in our communities know and love God, and this helps them lead with His **wisdom** and joy.
8. Proverbs 3:5 says to "Trust in the **LORD** with all your heart, and lean not on your own understanding. . . ."
9. We become a citizen of heaven when we believe in Him (Jesus), and we show that we are citizens of heaven by **loving** one another.

Follow the Language Time countries on the map from Lessons 10–18

Clipper Ships and Citizenships

Character Counts

LESSON #10

TEACHER NOTES

Developmental Mile Markers

Positive Reinforcement: Be positive with children in the way you provide encouragement by commenting on good behavior, realize that little steps are still steps, and know what each child needs in the way of reinforcement. This will help provide them with a model of good character.

Lesson Goals

Students should be able to:

- Recognize how important it is that we live like Christ in the world, demonstrating His love and godly character even when we are young.

SUPPLIES

- ☐ Crayons or colored pens or pencils

Character: A word that tells us about who we are and how we act.

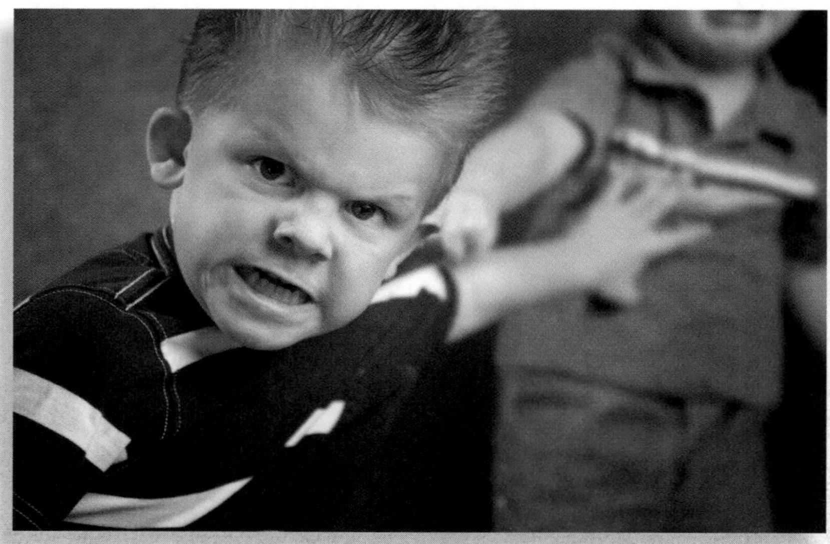

Name

Go time!

We're starting a new quest today. Come on, it's go time!

Character is a word that talks about who we are and how we act. The Bible teaches us that we can choose kindness and patience, that we can forgive others when they hurt us (Colossians 3:12, 13). So when we see how others act toward others, or see how we act toward others, know that all of us are making choices.

If someone acts mean on a Tuesday, it's possible that something upset them in the morning, and they were acting that way because their heart was hurting. But if someone acts mean every day of the week, then it is more likely that they are simply choosing to be mean. Just like if someone is kind every day of the week, we can know they are choosing to be kind. Either of these shows that person's **character**. The Bible teaches us that we are to look to Christ as our example, to treat others with kindness and goodness the way that He did.

God's Scripture time

Each week for this second quest, you will be remembering the Bible verses we learned in the first quest and spending more time memorizing them. Remember to look over your God's Scripture Time flashcards you put in your *My Story K* suitcase! We are talking about being citizens in this second quest, and this verse helps us know that our strength and abilities to love and live come from Christ! Now listen to this one again, then say it with me:

I can do all things through Christ who strengthens me (Philippians 4:13).

Language time!

07:00

Some people in the world speak a language called French. If you want to say "thank you" in French, you just say *merci* (mare see). Let's say it now, in a singing voice: *merci*. There are people in a country called the Democratic Republic of Congo who speak this language. Why don't you get your continent map of Africa and color in the Democratic Republic of Congo!

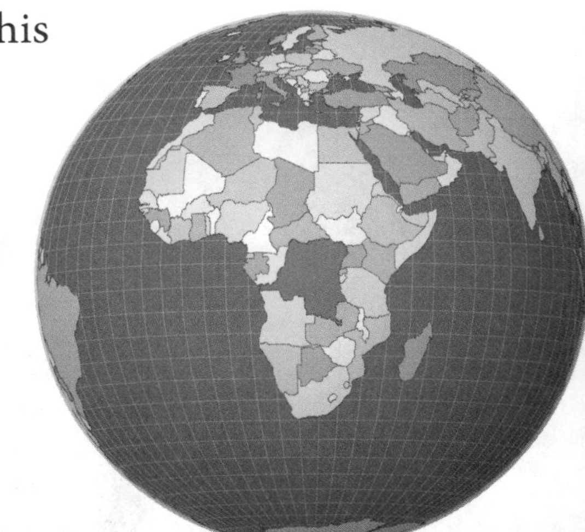

Name ________________________________

Picture time!

Winter Holidays and Festivals Around the World: All around the world, people celebrate Christmas, the birth of Jesus, the Son of God. Chinese New Year welcomes the New Year sometime between January and February in China. N'cwala is in February and celebrates the Ngoni tribe coming into Zambia back in 1835. Purim is in February and is celebrated by Jews around the world to honor Queen Esther, who saved the Jewish people from the evil Haman.

Color the winter image below.

Helping hands time!

Character is a word to describe the person you are, the kinds of choices you make, and the way you care about and love others or choose to hurt others. We choose to make good choices or bad choices, and we choose if we want to live our best for God. There are many people in our community who help us live better lives and make wise choices, including children's pastors, youth workers, and Sunday school teachers. God also brings other wise people into our lives to help guide us, including moms and dads, aunts and uncles, and grandparents.

Talk time!

Hopefully, most people in your life are good and kind people. What do you think are the things that make people seem good, the way Christ would have us be? What are the best things about your **character**?

My Book time!

Turn to the Lesson 10 My Book Time page in the back of this book to complete your story for the week in words and colors!

Driving in a Car, Look Where Laws Are Keeping Us Safe

LESSON #11

TEACHER NOTES

Developmental Mile Markers

Healthy Moral Growth: You can help children develop healthy moral guidelines by teaching them both the rules and why rules are important, making sure if they break rules that there is an appropriate consequence, and praising them in public and correcting them in private when possible. Understanding the nature of rules makes the understanding of laws a little easier.

SUPPLIES

- ☐ Crayons or colored pens or pencils

Lesson Goals

Students should be able to:

- Identify why various rules and laws exist and how they are meant to keep us safe.

word collector **Laws**: Rules to follow that are often created to keep us safe.

Name

MY STORY K
Lesson 11
Exercise 1 Day 1

Go time!

This week we're learning about **laws**. Get ready, get set, it's go time!

When we play games, there are always rules to follow, just as there are often rules in our homes. **Laws** serve a similar purpose to rules. **Laws** are created for many reasons, but one main reason is to keep people safe from harm.

Governments make **laws**, and everyone must follow them. Lots of signs are made to show us the **laws** or to show us dangers that we should avoid. They are meant to help keep us from getting hurt. Can you name some of the signs on this page or tell where you might find them? There are hundreds of **laws** in most any country, and there are certainly not hundreds of signs to tell us about them, but the signs do help us begin to understand them!

God's Scripture time

Get your God's Scripture Time flashcards ready! We are talking about keeping safe in this lesson, and this verse helps us know that we don't need to live fearfully because God is with us! Now listen to this one again, then say it with me:

Fear not, for I am with you . . . (Isaiah 43:5).

Language time!

Some people in the world speak a language called German. If you want to say "thank you" in German, you just say *danke* (dawn ka). Let's say it now, softly: *danke*. There are people in a country called Namibia who speak this language. Why don't you get your continent map of Africa and color in Namibia!

Name

Picture time!

Take some time to color the pictures of the different kinds of signs that help to keep you from harm. Can you pick out the sign for poison? For fire? For a stop sign? For a construction area? What should you do when you see these signs?

Helping hands time!

The next time you are in a car, van, or bus going around town, look at all the special signs put up to try to keep you safe. These include stop signs, yield signs, stop lights, and more. There are a lot of helpers who make sure the roads in your town are kept up, as well as make sure homes and businesses are safe. City workers and city council groups make sure communities are cared for, sheriffs help protect people on the roads, and social workers provide help to people struggling with needs at home.

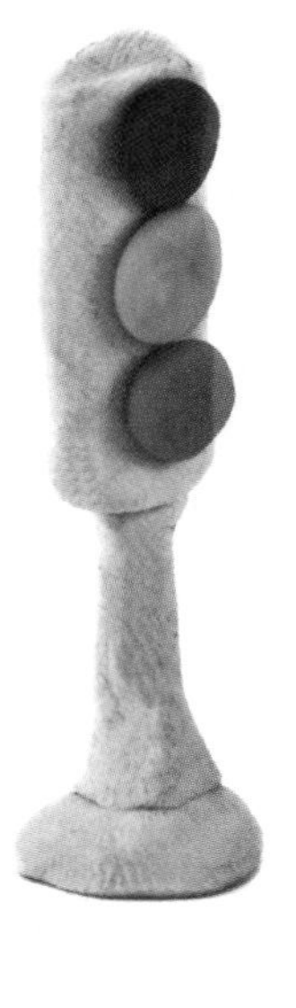

Talk time!

It seems like there are so many rules and laws we have to follow, but many of them are meant to keep us safe. What rules were you taught that keep you from harm?

My Book time!

Turn to the Lesson 11 My Book Time page in the back of this book to complete your story for the week in words and colors!

Skiing Slopes Safely

God Protects Us

LESSON #12

TEACHER NOTES

Developmental Mile Markers

Healthy Sleep: You can help children at night by creating night traditions and filling evenings with peace. And as they come to know God more in your home, they will come to know that His peace is greater than any fear.

Lesson Goals

Students should be able to:

- Discuss how God's guidance and laws help us know the difference between right and wrong.

SUPPLIES

- ☐ Crayons or colored pens or pencils
- ☐ Scissors
- ☐ Glue or tape (optional)

word collector **Protect**: To try to keep someone from being hurt.

Name ____________________

MY STORY K
Lesson 12
Exercise 1 Day 1

Go time!

It's time now to think about how good God is, keeping us safe in His love. That's right, it's go time!

God not only created the world and everything in space, but He created us to live in the world, and He watches over us to **protect** us and to show His love for us. He created the world to be the special place we grow in. And growing up isn't just about getting taller. We continue to grow even after we've stopped growing taller because our minds and hearts are always growing. Just as you are learning in this book about social studies and how God made the world, you will be learning all your life about being more and more the person God created you to be. You also learn to trust in God's goodness and in how He will protect you to provide all you need to be more like His Son, Jesus.

God's Scripture time

Get your God's Scripture Time flashcards ready! We are talking about how God can **protect** us in this lesson, and you'll remember how this verse shows us to be kind and forgiving like He is. We don't need to be afraid of things because God is watching over us, and that means we can be good to people around us. Now listen to this one again, then say it with me:

And be kind to one another, tenderhearted, forgiving one another, even as God in Christ forgave you (Ephesians 4:32).

Language time!

Some people in the world speak a language called Hawaiian. If you want to say "thank you" in Hawaiian, you just say *mahalo* (ma ha low). Let's say it now, in a big voice: *mahalo*. There are people in a state called Hawaii that is a part of the United States who speak this language. Why don't you get your continent map of North America and color in Hawaii!

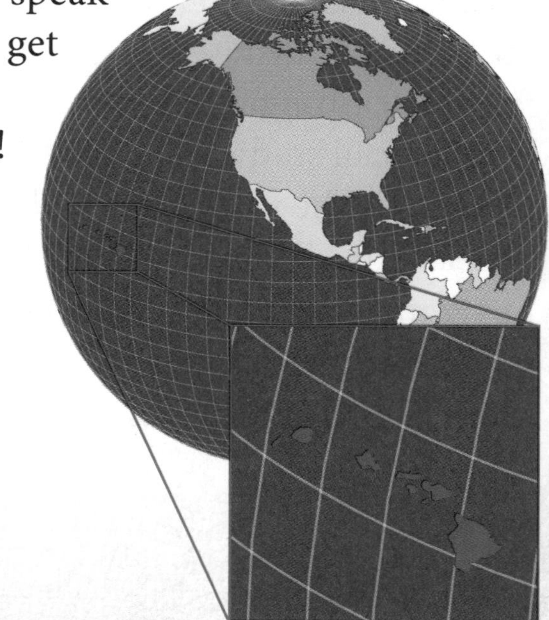

Name

Picture time!

Cut out the snowman and all the things you can use to dress him up to protect him from the cold. You can either glue/tape the pieces to another paper or keep them in a small bag to use again and again. Your teacher can help you if you need any help at all.

Page blank for cutting purposes.

Helping hands time!

No matter where you go in the world, God is with you to **protect** you and keep you safe. And God makes sure there are people around us to keep us safe, as well. There are those in your own family who pray for you and watch over you when you're young, including parents, grandparents, cousins, and more. And in churches, God makes sure to provide lots of people who care for us and our families, including pastors, elders, deacons, and teachers, as well as those who help provide food and clothing to those in need. If you ever feel afraid of something, go to someone God has placed in your life to keep you safe.

Talk time!

God is so good to us. He provides for us, cares for us, watches over us. Do you have a favorite Bible account where it shows how God could **protect** His people (like Noah or Daniel or Mary and Joseph)?

My Book time!

Turn to the Lesson 12 My Book Time page in the back of this book to complete your story for the week in words and colors!

Cable Cars and Customs Near and Far

Traditions Around the World

LESSON #13

TEACHER NOTES

Developmental Mile Markers

Healthy Social Connections: You can help children develop healthy social connections by encouraging playtime with friends, developing a healthy respect for friends and their things, and helping them know that sometimes friends get sad or angry. Seeing how a friend's family might have slightly different traditions can help a child discover the bigger differences in cultures around the world.

SUPPLIES

- ☐ Crayons or colored pens or pencils

Lesson Goals

Students should be able to:

- Compare and contrast various traditions and customs of cultures around the world.

word collector **Traditions**: A belief we act out and pass down to our families.

Family making cookies on Christmas Eve

Vietnamese family in traditional clothing

Indian family in traditional clothing

Name

Go time!

I hope you're ready for another adventure because it's go time!

Traditions or customs are events that are important for us and followed over the course of time. This might be something simple, like praying over your nightly dinner, or something more worldwide for followers of Christ, like celebrating Christmas. We were made by God to have a relationship with Him. These customs and **traditions** can help us remember His goodness to us and to be thankful to Him for all He does. There are actually hundreds and hundreds of holiday **traditions** celebrated around the world. Many nations celebrate the New Year's holiday on January 1. And though many nations also celebrate their country's independence day, these are all celebrated on different days because they are like country birthdays. Take some time to look up resources on holidays around the world if you're interested in exploring more!

Family members like to get together on Christmas

Get your God's Scripture Time flashcards ready! We are talking about **traditions** around the world in this lesson, and you'll remember how this verse talks about how we are wonderfully made by God. And just as He made us so marvelously, so He made everyone else in the world, though so many don't yet know Him to praise Him like we do. Now listen to this one again, then say it with me:

I will praise You, for I am fearfully and wonderfully made; marvelous are Your works, and that my soul knows very well (Psalm 139:14).

Language 07:00 time!

Some people in the world speak a language called Hebrew. If you want to say "thank you" in Hebrew, you just say *todah* (toh dah). Let's say it now, in a little voice: *todah*. There are people in a country called Israel who speak this language. Why don't you get your continent map of Asia and color in Israel!

Jewish sisters celebrating Hanukkah

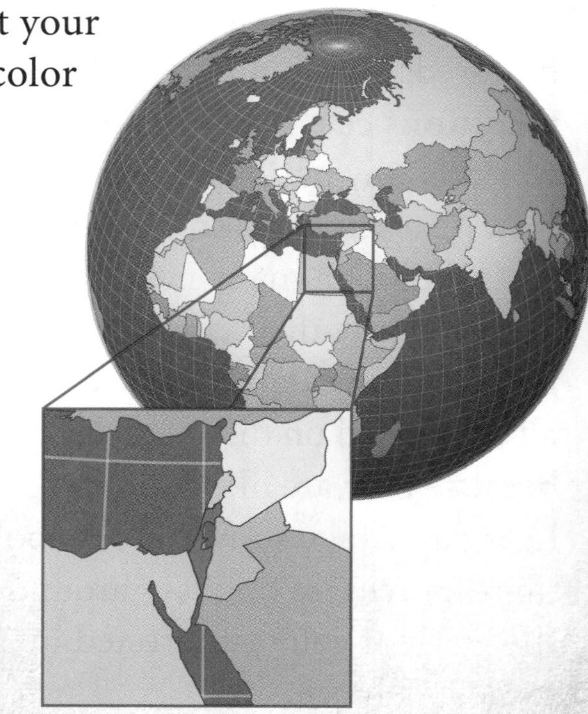

Name

MY STORY K
Lesson 13
Exercise 2 Day 2

Picture time!

Color the picture of the nativity scene.

Helping hands time!

One day you might get to travel around the world and see different customs and **traditions**. If you do get to go, there are a lot of helpers that will be there to get you to your next stop! Getting from place to place in a city, you may just need a taxi driver or a bus driver. If you have to go across a state, a territory, or a province, you might need a train engineer. And if you want to go from country to country, you'll probably need an airplane pilot.

Talk time!

Traditions that we celebrate each year help us feel connected to those we celebrate with, like family time at Thanksgiving or Christmas. But just having dinner with your family each night can be a tradition. What are some of your favorite family **traditions**?

My Book time!

Turn to the Lesson 13 My Book Time page in the back of this book to complete your story for the week in words and colors!

Riding a Funicular with Friends

My Friends and Me

LESSON #14

TEACHER NOTES

Developmental Mile Markers

Height and Weight: An average boy at age 5 is 43 inches tall and 40½ pounds, while the average girl at age 5 is 42½ inches tall and 39¾ pounds. Note that an average only shows the mid-range of children, with some being smaller and some larger. Each child develops in many ways and always at their own pace, so we can teach our children to be patient if they sense they are different from their friends.

SUPPLIES

- ☐ Crayons or colored pens or pencils

Lesson Goals

Students should be able to:

- Define friendships and how important it is for us to have godly friends to lift us up.

Friends: People we like to spend time with who often like what we like.

Name

Go time!

A week to ride funiculars with **friends**? That's right, it's go time!

Friends are those people we like to spend time with, who like a lot of the same things we do, and who often believe similar things to us. The best **friends** are those who pray with us and for us, who are patient and kind, and who make us feel God's joy in the time we share with them. In the Bible (Proverbs 18:24), we are told that someone who has **friends** must be friendly. This includes being supportive of our **friends**, being kind to them, being patient with them, and being loving and forgiving with them. Do you show this kind of character with your **friends**?

Draw or color what your friend might see out this window.

Get your God's Scripture Time flashcards ready! We are talking about **friends** in this lesson, and you'll remember how this verse talks about how we can rejoice in the Lord at all times. When our hearts are always rejoicing in the Lord, our friendships will be stronger and happier. Now listen to this one again, then say it with me:

Rejoice in the Lord always. Again I will say, rejoice! (Philippians 4:4).

Language time!

Some people in the world speak a language called Hindi. If you want to say "thank you" in Hindi, you just say *dhanyavad* (dawn ya vahd). Let's say it now, calmly: *dhanyavad*. There are people in a country called India who speak this language. Why don't you get your continent map of Asia and color in India!

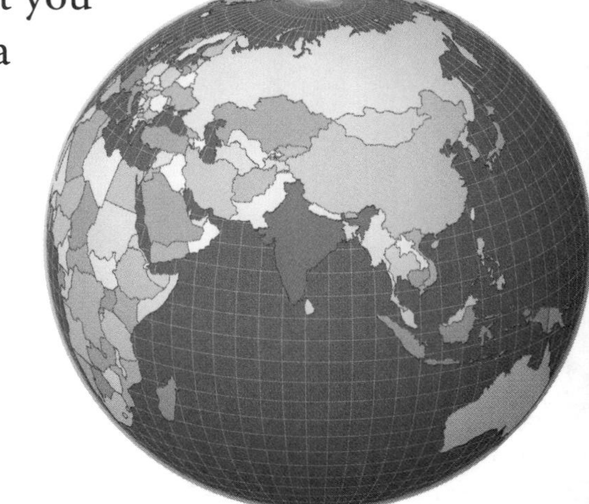

Name

Picture time!

Color the picture of friends playing.

There are a lot of people in the world, but those people we call **friends** come the closest to being like our family. **Friends** often have a lot of the same likes and dislikes we have, they often make us smile and laugh, and they tend to love us just as we are. You might find good **friends** in a special group you are a part of, at your church, or perhaps you have some neighbors that have become **friends**. But wherever you find a good friend, be thankful!

Friends are such wonderful gifts from God! What are some of the best things about a good friend? Are you like this for those who call you their friend? How can you show a good friend you are thankful for him or her?

Turn to the Lesson 14 My Book Time page in the back of this book to complete your story for the week in words and colors!

On a Bus with All of Us

Resolving Conflict

LESSON #15

TEACHER NOTES

Developmental Mile Markers

Coping with Conflict: Family conflicts will certainly happen, but you can learn to make even conflict a learning tool. Know that all families argue, but how the individuals of each family respond can be very different. Try to keep calm during conflicts, listening carefully to each person involved, and make sure the tone is always rooted in love. Model healthy discussion.

Lesson Goals

Students should be able to:

- Explain certain ways we can let love guide our families and friendships in order to avoid hurting others or losing control when we are upset.

SUPPLIES

- ☐ Crayons or colored pens or pencils

word collector **Conflict**: When we fight with our family or friends.

Name

Go time!

Hop on the bus! It's go time!

We like to have happy days where everyone gets along, but sometimes we get angry or upset. When we fight with those in our family, or with people we work with when we get older, it is called **conflict**. These things happen no matter how hard we try to keep away from them, but we can do things to help fix the conflict and to create peace again.

One of the most important things you can do when there is **conflict** is to stop and understand why you or the other person might be upset. So pausing to listen and talking calmly really can help. Sometimes you might have to talk about a problem to come up with a way to fix it together. Try and be fair when talking about problems. Also, sometimes you can talk about a pretend problem to learn how you might solve a real problem. Definitely practice saying "I'm sorry," because it isn't always easy to say!

God's Scripture time

Get your God's Scripture Time flashcards ready! We are talking about resolving **conflict** in this lesson, and you'll remember how this verse talks about loving our neighbors. When we honor God by loving others as He wants us to, we will find ways of bringing peace at times when family or friends might be fighting. Now listen to this one again, then say it with me:

You shall love your neighbor as yourself (Matthew 22:39).

Language time!

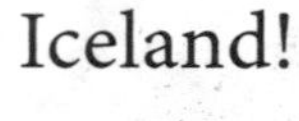

Some people in the world speak a language called Icelandic. If you want to say "thank you" in Icelandic, you just say *takk* (taw ck). Let's say it now, smiling: *takk*. There are people in a country called Iceland who speak this language. Why don't you get your continent map of Europe and color in Iceland!

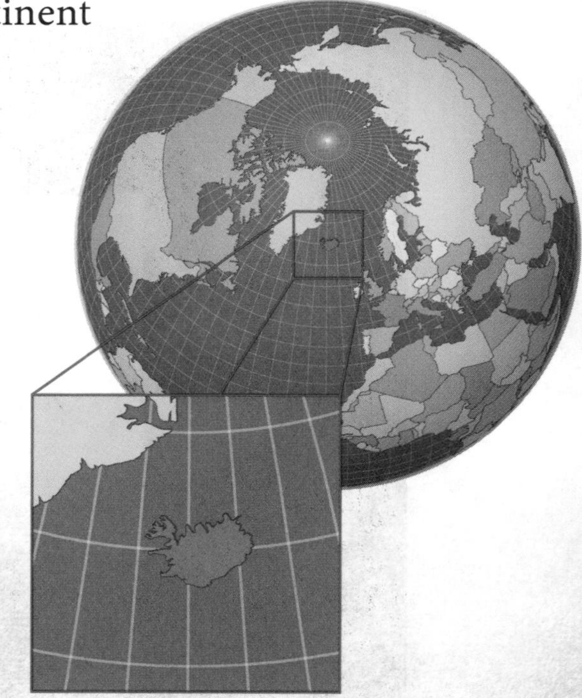

Name ______________________________

Picture time!

Circle these 12 hidden objects in the picture below.

Now circle these sea creatures. Look closely. Some are hiding!

Sometimes we argue or fight with those we love. Sometimes we argue or fight with our friends. No matter how hard we try to love and be kind, there are just times we get angry or frustrated, and sometimes we need other people God sends to us to help us better see things the way He sees them. These helpers include people called counselors who talk with us about things that hurt our feelings, managers of workplaces who help guide us into jobs that give us more joy, and sign language translators who help people in the deaf community share their needs with those who do not know how to speak sign language.

The Bible is filled with accounts of people fighting against each other and against God. This comes with our sin nature. But we are able to find peace because of the love of Jesus. What do you think you can do to help bring peace to your family and friends?

Turn to the Lesson 15 My Book Time page in the back of this book to complete your story for the week in words and colors!

Jets with Wings for Mayors and Kings

Community Leaders

LESSON #16

TEACHER NOTES

Developmental Mile Markers

Teaching Through Example: With younger children, remember to model politeness, being courteous to other people, including saying things like "please" and "thank you." Be positive with specific directions, always being constructive and encouraging, and limit the number of directions you give a child at any one time. This kindness will become a part of their character as they grow into leadership roles as adults.

SUPPLIES

- ☐ Crayons or colored pens or pencils

Lesson Goals

Students should be able to:

- Describe various leaders in their community and in the world.

word collector **Leaders**: Those who lead people to be the best at whatever they do.

Name

Go time!

There are lots of things to see this week. Come on, it's go time!

Every community has **leaders**, whether it is a large or small community. Most towns and cities have mayors who lead them. Who are your local **leaders**, including pastors and community **leaders**? Your teacher can certainly help you! And who is your president, prime minister, or other leader of your country? Take a moment right now to pray for your **leaders**. They face so many hard times trying to help and support as many people in the nation as possible.

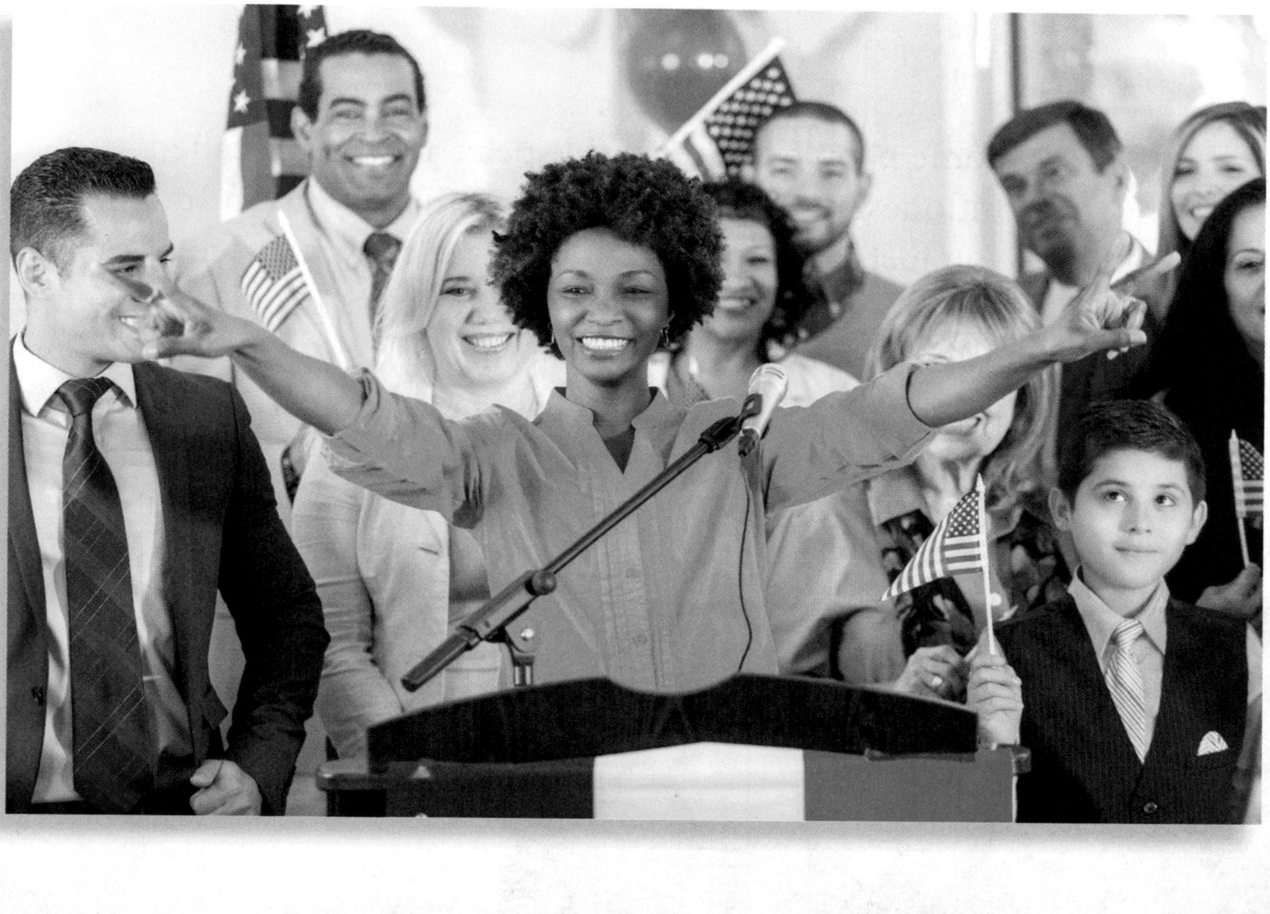

God's Scripture time

Get your God's Scripture Time flashcards ready! We are talking about community leaders in this lesson, and you'll remember how this verse talks about loving God and others by keeping His commandments. Many who serve in our communities know and love God, and this helps them lead with His wisdom and joy. Now listen to this one again, then say it with me:

For this is the love of God, that we keep His commandments. And His commandments are not burdensome (1 John 5:3).

Language time!

Some people in the world speak a language called Indonesian. If you want to say "thank you" in Indonesian, you just say *terima kasih* (tuh-ree-mah kah-see). Let's say it now, bashfully: *terima kasih*. There are people in a country called Indonesia who speak this language. Why don't you get your continent map of Asia and color in Indonesia!

Name

Picture time!

What kind of tool do you think I need to do my job? Draw a line from the worker to the tool that is important to them.

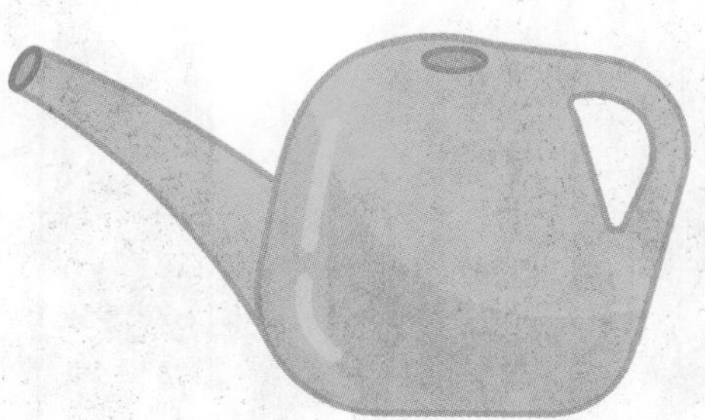

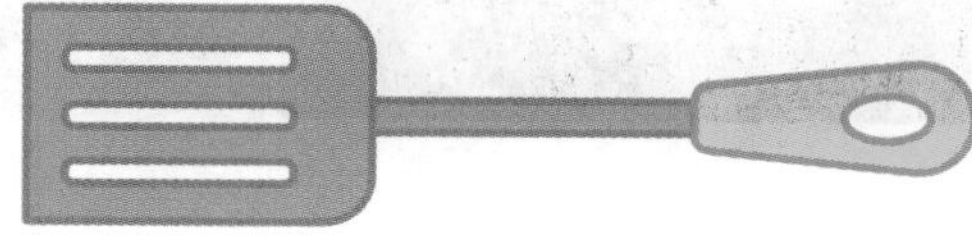

Every community in the world has special **leaders** who try to make sure that their people are safe and have all the resources they need to live happy and healthy lives. Many cities in the world are led by mayors, many states or provinces are led by governors or premiers, and many countries are led by presidents, prime ministers, chancellors, chairmen, or kings and queens. So many titles for so many helpers!

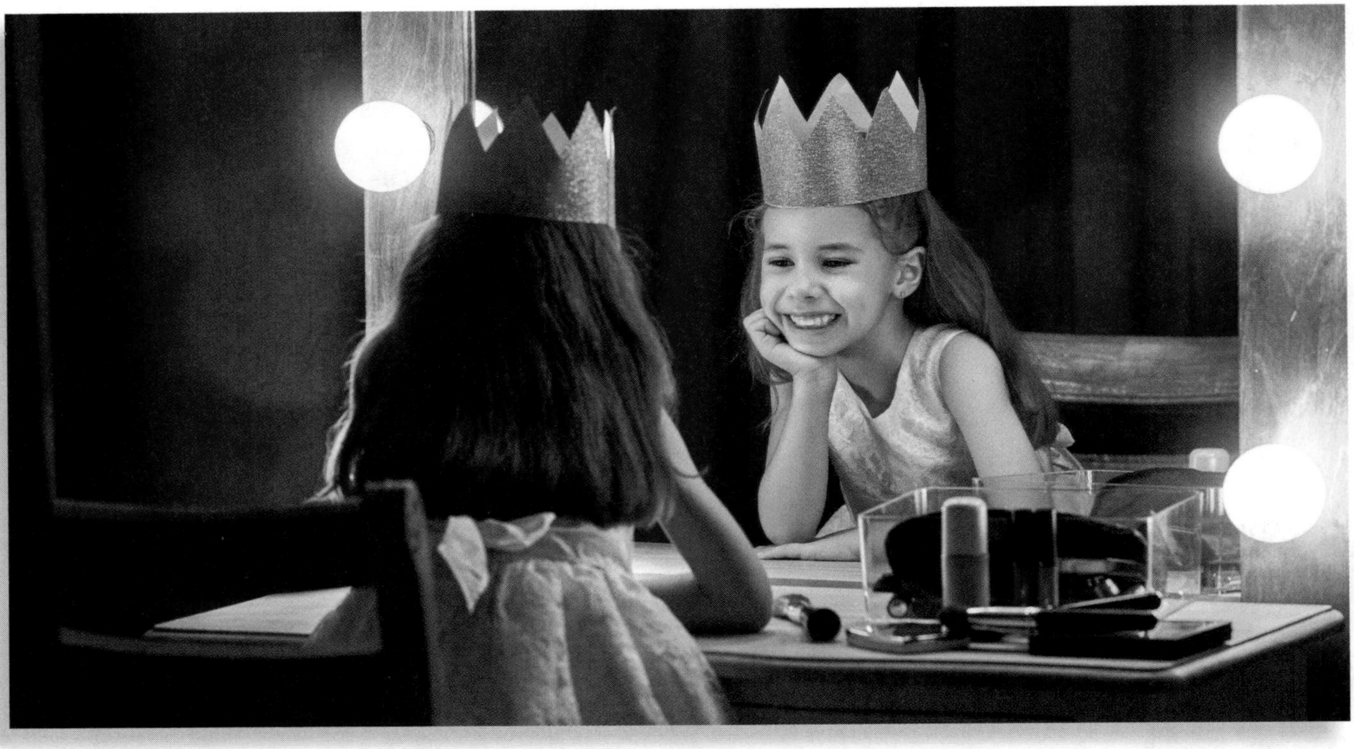

Leaders help guide small towns, as well as whole countries! Do you or your family know any **leaders** in your community? If people wanted you to lead them one day, what kind of leader would you hope to be?

Turn to the Lesson 16 My Book Time page in the back of this book to complete your story for the week in words and colors!

On Braces, Up Ladders, to Do What Really Matters

Heroes and Helpers

LESSON #17

TEACHER NOTES

Developmental Mile Markers

Healthy Moral Growth: You can help children develop healthy moral guidelines by explaining to them about God's love and wisdom for all of us and modeling love and kindness as much as possible. It is often a strong Christlike character that will set apart heroes and helpers.

Lesson Goals

Students should be able to:

- Recognize various heroes and helpers in their communities and how these people make sure it is a good world for us.

Heroes: People who work hard to make the world better and safer for others.

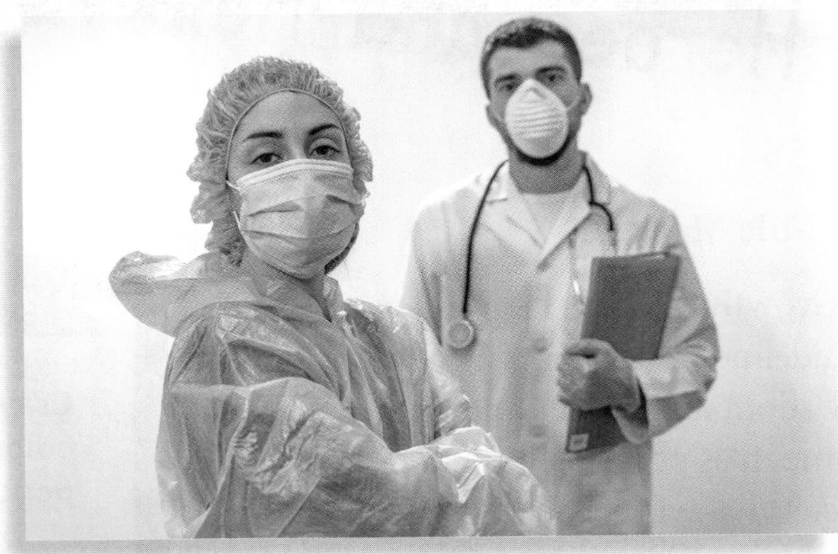

Name ______________________

Go time!

We've got another week to share! It's go time!

We're talking about **heroes** and helpers this week, and we can be thankful that they are everywhere! We often think of amazing firemen, policemen, and hospital workers who help save lives and keep us safe. And yet there are so many more. Let's think about this for just a few moments. There are also moms and dads and grandparents, grocery workers, and those who work on electric lines. So many people work to help others and to support others, and so they are truly **heroes** too.

God's Scripture time

Get your God's Scripture Time flashcards ready! We are talking about heroes and helpers in this lesson, and you'll remember how this verse tells us to trust in the Lord and not our own understanding. Heroes and helpers in your community would show such wisdom to trust in the Lord too. He can help them with all they need to know and help them make good choices. Now listen to this one again, then say it with me:

Trust in the LORD *with all your heart, and lean not on your own understanding . . .* (Proverbs 3:5).

Language time!

Some people in the world speak a language called Italian. If you want to say "thank you" in Italian, you just say *grazie* (graht tsyeh). Let's say it now, quickly: *grazie*. There are people in a country called Italy who speak this language. Why don't you get your continent map of Europe and color in Italy!

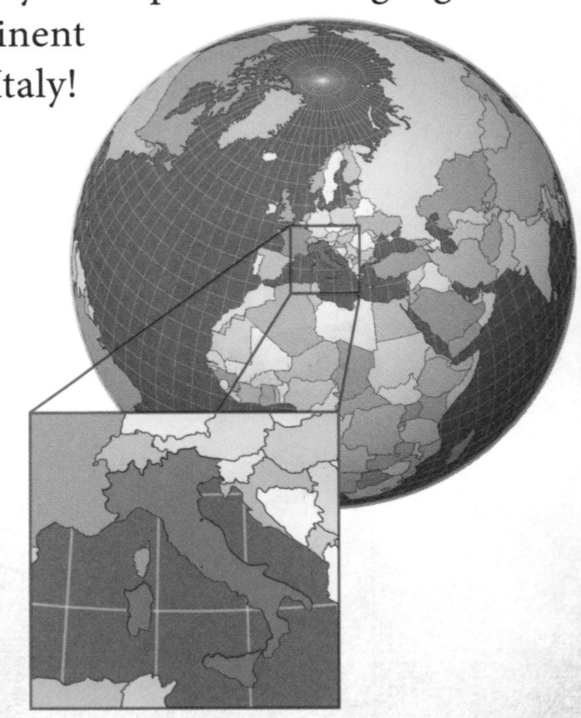

Name

Picture time!

Draw a line to connect the helper with the object they use.

Helping hands time!

We know that there are **heroes** and helpers all around us. Some we recognize as wonderful, and some are more quiet **heroes**, but God has placed them everywhere. There are some you'll find at hospitals working at the front desk, or the nurses who care for you, or the doctors who make sure you are well. And there are those who work all hours of the day and night at grocery stores to make sure you can get good things to eat and drink, as well as bank workers who make sure your money is kept safe and to make sure you can have the money you need to buy your home.

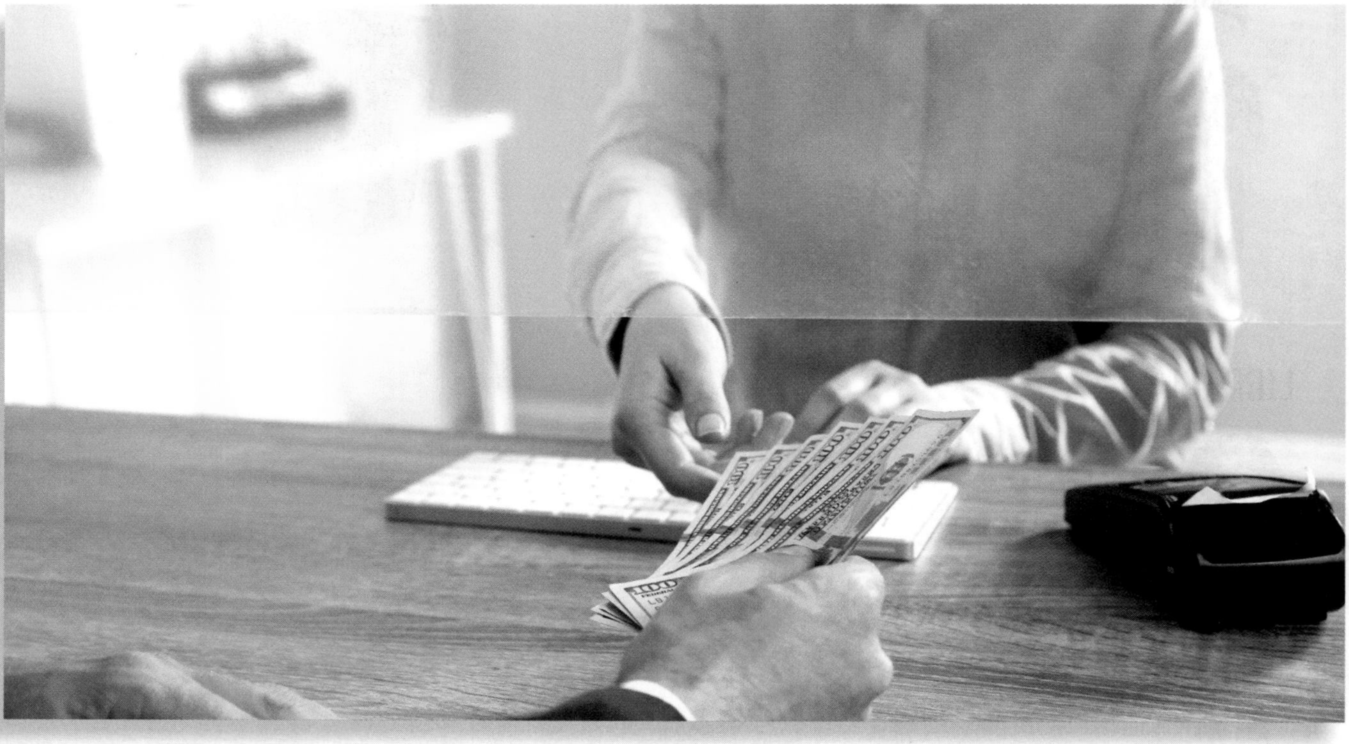

Heroes come in all shapes and sizes, and they might be young or old, but they all do heroic things. What do you think of when you hear the word "hero"?

Turn to the Lesson 17 My Book Time page in the back of this book to complete your story for the week in words and colors!

Citizens of Heaven

LESSON #18

TEACHER NOTES

End of week recipe ingredients:

- ☐ 2 cups filtered apple juice
- ☐ 1 pound Gruyere cheese, shredded
- ☐ 2 tablespoons cornstarch
- ☐ ¼ cup grated Parmesan cheese
- ☐ ½ teaspoon grainy Dijon mustard
- ☐ Salt and ground black pepper
- ☐ Cubed bread, cubed meat, or veggies

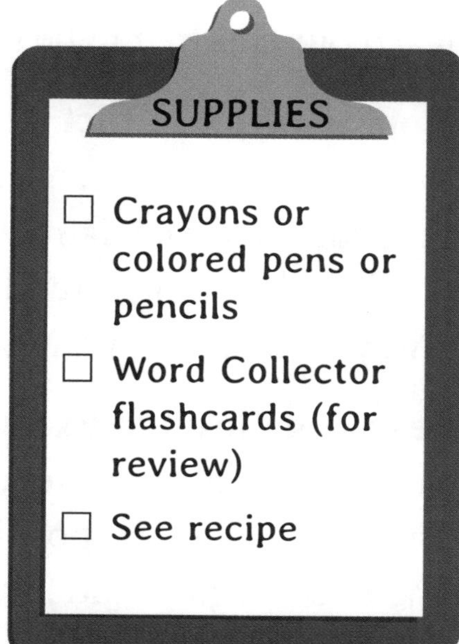

Developmental Mile Markers Review

Positive Reinforcement: Be positive with children in the way you provide encouragement by commenting on good behavior, realize that little steps are still steps, and know what each child needs in the way of reinforcement. This will help provide them with a model of good character.

Healthy Moral Growth: You can help children develop healthy moral guidelines by teaching them both the rules and why rules are important, making sure if they break rules that there is an appropriate consequence, and praising them in public and correcting them in private when possible. Understanding the nature of rules makes the understanding of laws a little easier.

Healthy Sleep: You can help children at night by creating night traditions and filling evenings with peace. And as they come to know God more in your home, they will come to know that His peace is greater than any fear.

Healthy Social Connections: You can help children develop healthy social connections by encouraging playtime with friends, developing a healthy respect for friends and their things, and helping them know that sometimes friends get sad or angry. Seeing how a friend's family might have slightly different traditions can help a child discover the bigger differences in cultures around the world.

Height and Weight: An average boy at age 5 is 43 inches tall and 40½ pounds, while the average girl at age 5 is 42½ inches tall and 39¾ pounds. Note that an average only shows the mid-range of children, with some being smaller and some larger. Each child develops in many ways and always at their own pace, so we can teach our children to be patient if they sense they are different from their friends.

Coping with Conflict: Family conflicts will certainly happen, but you can learn to make even conflict a learning tool. Know that all families argue, but how the individuals of each family respond can be very different. Try to keep calm during conflicts, listening carefully to each person involved, and make sure the tone is always rooted in love. Model healthy discussion.

Teaching Through Example: With younger children, remember to model politeness, being courteous to other people, including saying things like "please" and "thank you." Be positive with specific directions, always being constructive and encouraging, and limit the number of directions you give a child at any one time. This kindness will become a part of their character as they grow into leadership roles as adults.

Healthy Moral Growth: You can help children develop healthy moral guidelines by explaining to them about God's love and wisdom for all of us and modeling love and kindness as much as possible. It is often a strong Christlike character that will set apart heroes and helpers.

Lesson Goals

Students should be able to:

- Define citizenship and how we are born citizens of a country and how we can become citizens of heaven.

Citizen: Someone who has special rights in his or her country.

Name ______

It's the end of another quest! Hop on the train, it's go time!

We're talking about being a **citizen** this week. A **citizen** is someone who has special rights and responsibilities in a particular country. How do you become a **citizen** of a country? Most people become a **citizen** of a country because they are born there. But there are other ways you can be made a **citizen** as well, including applying to be a **citizen** and waiting to complete the process through classes and approvals. Being a **citizen** means you have certain protections under the law because you have a special place in the country. For Christians, those who are saved by grace through faith, we become citizens of heaven as well. This means we have special responsibilities in God's eyes. And He gives us special rights because we become His children.

God's Scripture time

Get your God's Scripture Time flashcards ready! We are talking about being a **citizen** of heaven in this lesson, and you'll remember how this verse talks about us believing on the name of Jesus and loving each other. We become a **citizen** of heaven when we believe in Him, and we show that we are citizens of heaven by loving one another. Now listen to this one again, then say it with me:

And this is His commandment: that we should believe on the name of His Son Jesus Christ and love one another, as He gave us commandment (1 John 3:23).

Language 07:00 time!

Some people in the world speak a language called Japanese. If you want to say "thank you" in Japanese, you just say *arigato* (a ree gat oh). Let's say it now, slowly: *arigato*. There are people in a country called Japan who speak this language. Why don't you get your continent map of Asia and color in Japan!

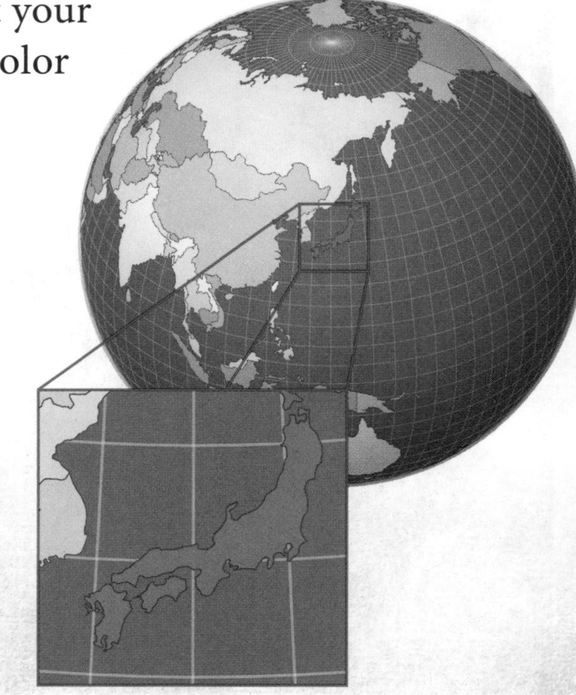

Name

Picture time!

Most people are born with what are called the five senses. These are sight, hearing, smell, taste, and touch. We see with our eyes, hear sound with our ears, smell with our nose, taste with our tongues, and feel touch through our skin. These are ways God created for us to experience His world. Sometimes people lose their vision and cannot see, or they are unable to hear or hear things muffled. We all have strengths and weaknesses, and God is able to help us do great things no matter what may seem to hinder us. Draw a line to connect the five senses to what they help you enjoy in the world.

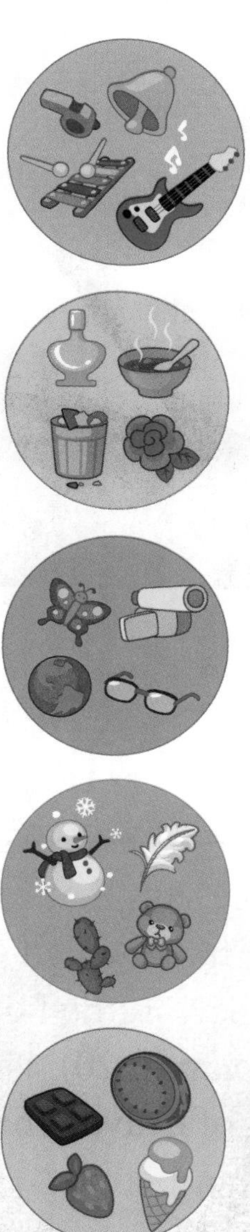

We are all born as citizens of a particular country on earth. That means we have certain rights and responsibilities as a **citizen**. But as you are learning, we become citizens of heaven when we accept God's gift of eternal life through Jesus. In communities around the world, God has put helpers who teach us what it means to be a good **citizen** of heaven. These include missionaries who go to places where few know of the love of Jesus, evangelists who share the good news of Jesus, disciples who try and be like Jesus, and teachers who help us learn and grow in God's grace.

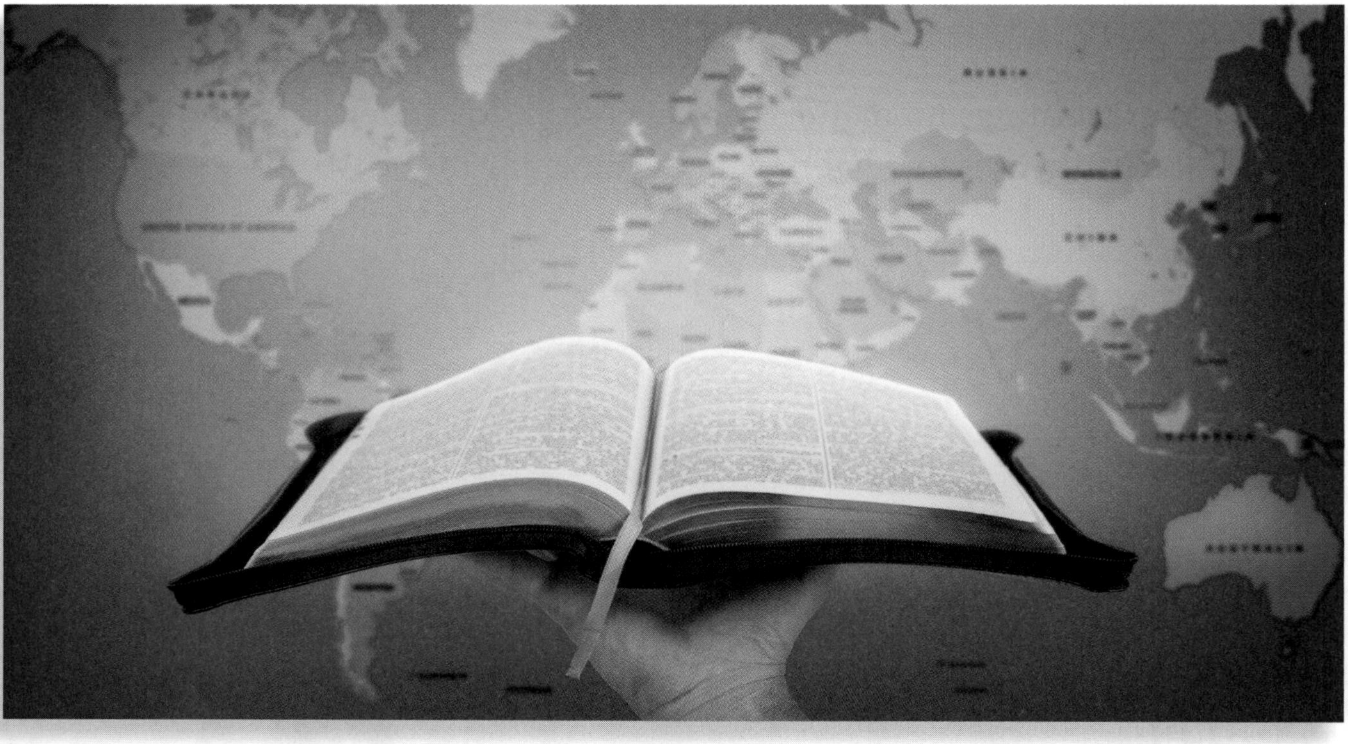

The Bible says that "our citizenship is in heaven, from which we also eagerly wait for the Savior, the Lord Jesus Christ" (Philippians 3:20). How do you think citizens of heaven might live differently than other people?

Turn to the Lesson 18 My Book Time page in the back of this book to complete your story for the week in words and colors!

Food Time

Cheeses Around the World!

Another staple around the world is cheese. Many countries and cultures have a particular kind of cheese or cheeses that are eaten often, if not every day. Cheese is made with milk — most often, cow's milk. There is also cheese made with sheep, goat, buffalo, and reindeer milk as well.

What types of cheeses do you have in your house? Do you eat cheese at breakfast? In your eggs or on toast? Do you have cheese for lunch in a sandwich or with pasta like macaroni? What about for a snack or at dinnertime? The next time you and your family go to the store or market this week, look for different kinds of cheeses. Try a cheese you've never tried before if you can.

Each year, the country of Greece eats the most cheese per person, while the United States makes the most cheese, and France sends more cheese to other nations than any other country.

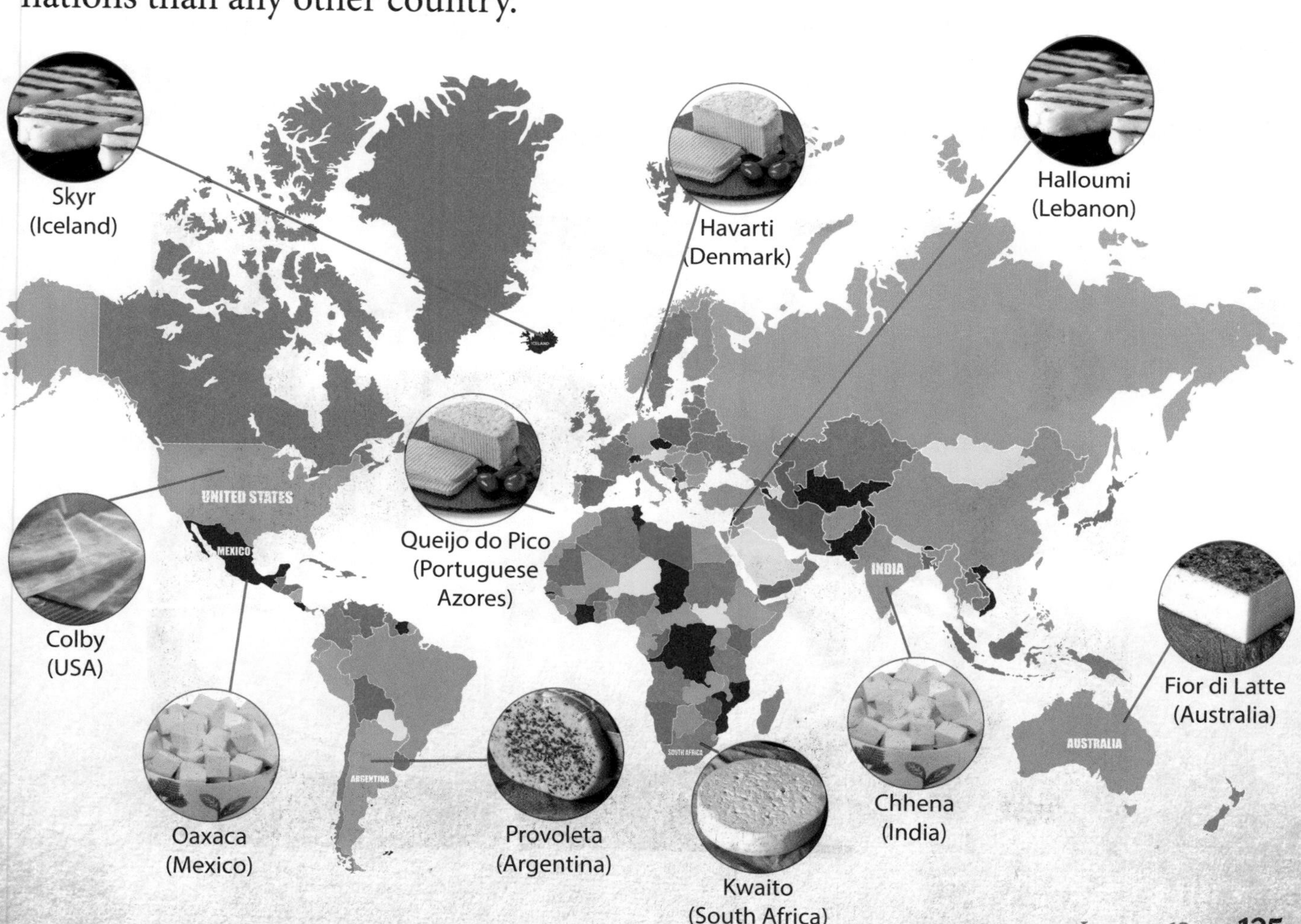

Here's a recipe to try and make with your teacher:

Cheese Fondue

Switzerland and France

Ingredients

- ☐ 2 cups filtered apple juice
- ☐ 1 pound Gruyere cheese, shredded
- ☐ 2 tablespoons cornstarch
- ☐ ¼ cup grated Parmesan cheese
- ☐ ½ teaspoon grainy Dijon mustard
- ☐ Salt and ground black pepper
- ☐ Dippers (cubed bread, cubed meat, or veggies)

In a medium saucepan, bring the apple juice to a simmer over medium heat. In a bowl or plastic zip-lock bag, toss the Gruyere and cornstarch to coat the cheese. While whisking, slowly add the cheese to the simmering apple juice. Whisk mixture continuously until smooth, allowing it to come to a boil in between additions. Remove from the heat, stir in the Parmesan and mustard, and season with ½ teaspoon salt and pepper to taste. Pour fondue into serving bowl. Serve with the dippers of your choice.

QUEST
TWO
CONGRATULATIONS!
Name
Finished Quest Two of *My Story K!*
Date

Quest Collector Card!

QUEST THREE

Tear out this page and circle the bolded words as you find them in the lessons!

1. The higher up you go in a plane or a rocket, the more of the world you see, until in space you look back and see the whole **earth** below you.
2. **Maps** are drawings that show cities, states, provinces, countries, and even the whole world.
3. Part of being a blessing to our community is being **kind**, having a tender heart, and forgiving each other.
4. Rural is a word that means in the country, and **urban** is a word that means in the city.
5. The **nation** you are from reflects your nationality, but it is only one part of what makes you *you*.
6. Matthew 22:39 says that "You shall **love** your neighbor as yourself."
7. One simple way we can show God's love is by providing **food** to people in need — directly, through our church, or through a local food pantry.
8. Geography is a word that means **writing** about the earth.
9. It shouldn't matter if it is sunny or stormy, our faith or belief in **Jesus** shouldn't change, and we should always be found loving others.

GREENLAND
CANADA
USA
MEXICO
CUBA
ICELAND
22
NORWAY
SWEDEN
FINLAND
20
UK
IRELAND
FRANCE
SPAIN
GERMANY
POLAND
BELARUS
UKRAINE
ITALY
27
GREECE
TURKEY
RUSSIA
26
KAZAKHSTAN
MONGOLIA
21
CHINA
19
JAPAN
TAIWAN
PHILIPPINES
IRAQ
IRAN
AFGHANISTAN
PAKISTAN
SAUDI ARABIA
YEMEN
24
INDIA
23
MALAYSIA
INDONESIA
AUSTRALIA
NEW ZEALAND
ALGERIA
LIBYA
EGYPT
MAURITANIA
MALI
NIGER
CHAD
SUDAN
SOUTH SUDAN
ETHIOPIA
SOMALIA
NIGERIA
CONGO (DEMOCRATIC REPUBLIC)
KENYA
TANZANIA
ANGOLA
ZAMBIA
NAMIBIA
SOUTH AFRICA
MADAGASCAR
VENEZUELA
COLOMBIA
PERU
25
BRAZIL
BOLIVIA
CHILE
ARGENTINA
W
E
NW
NE
SW
SE
Follow the Language
Time countries on the
map from Lessons 19–27

I'll Walk and Roam Over All My Home

Local Life

LESSON #19

TEACHER NOTES

Developmental Mile Markers

Healthy Activity: You can help children keep active by having them choose sports they like, keep active with your family, or find enjoyment in activity each day. And whether you live in the city or country, getting outside whenever you can helps keep you connected to God's wondrous creation.

Lesson Goals

Students should be able to:

- Explain what life is like in the countryside or city in which they live.

SUPPLIES

- ☐ Crayons or colored pens or pencils

word collector **Neighbor**: A person who lives near our home.

Name

Go time!

Let's go on another quest! It's go time!

Go outside and look around. What do you see? Do you see houses around yours, or hills, or trees? If you could go up in a really tall building or climb a really tall tree, what might you see? The higher up you go in a plane or a rocket, the more of the world you see, until in space you look back and see the whole earth below you. God made the world for our home!

Now, if you live in the city, it's more likely you have a good **neighbor** next door to you on your street. You also might be able to get to stores and shops fairly quickly. If you live in the country, your closest **neighbor** and stores might be a few miles away, but you probably have lots of space for growing fruits and vegetables or to have lots of animals. Either way, there are blessings God provides wherever you call home!

Each week for this third quest, you will be going back over the Bible verses you learned in the first quest and seeing if we have memorized them yet. Remember to look over your God's Scripture Time flashcards you put in your *My Story K* suitcase! We are talking about God's world in this third quest, and this verse helps us know that no matter what happens in the world, Christ gives us the ability to do all we need to do. Now listen to this one again, then say it with me:

I can do all things through Christ who strengthens me (Philippians 4:13).

Language 07:00 time!

Some people in the world speak a language called Korean. If you want to say "thank you" in Korean, you just say *kamsahamnida* (come sam nee dah). Let's say it now, shyly: *kamsahamnida*. There are people in a country called South Korea who speak this language. Why don't you get your continent map of Asia and color in South Korea!

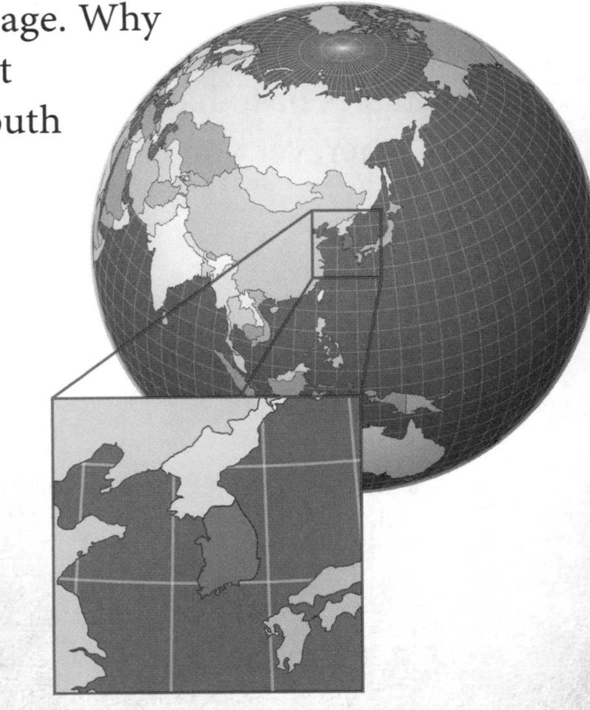

Name

Picture time!

Color in the things in the picture that you might see at or near your home!

Helping hands time!

In small towns and big cities, there are helpers who make sure that people are cared for and that work is done so there is money to buy food, clothing, and housing. Some of these people work as hotel clerks who make sure travelers have a place to stay, servers who make sure travelers have warm food to eat, and maids who make sure rooms are clean for travelers to find rest. There are also factory workers in many communities who process food or who make clothing and other items to make sure our towns and cities can be supported through the money that is made as these items are sold around the world.

Talk time!

Wherever you happen to live when you grow up, you will have memories that last a lifetime! What memories do you have of your life so far that you never want to forget? Why are these so special for you?

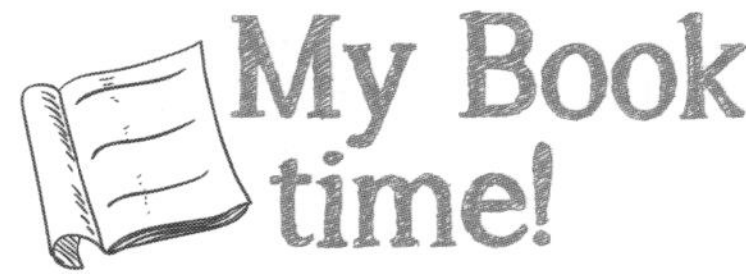

My Book time!

Turn to the Lesson 19 My Book Time page in the back of this book to complete your story for the week in words and colors!

On a Glider at Day Finding My Way

Maps

LESSON #20

TEACHER NOTES

Developmental Mile Markers

Fine Motor Skills: Children 4 to 5 years old should be able to copy some shapes, use a spoon and fork, and use scissors to cut on lines. All these skills will help children discern the varied shapes and lines on maps so they can tell roads from rivers and more.

Lesson Goals

Students should be able to:

- Identify the basic elements of a map, including various features regarding directions and the map key.

SUPPLIES

- ☐ Crayons or colored pens or pencils

Maps: Drawings that show roads and cities, and sometimes rivers and mountains.

Name ______________________

Time to learn more about God's world. That's right, it's go time!

Maps are drawings that show cities, states, provinces, countries, and even the whole world. Some just show streets, while others show buildings, rivers and forests, or other features.

There are four main directions you can find when looking at **maps**. These are north, south, east, and west. If you look at the map, you can know that right is east, left is west, up is north, and down is south. Below is a map that shows the seven continents of the earth. Continents are large areas of land that often have lots of countries on them. Have your teacher read some of the names and see how many you can say back. Then look at the continent that you live on. Oh, one other thing — globes are maps of the world that are round, like the earth!

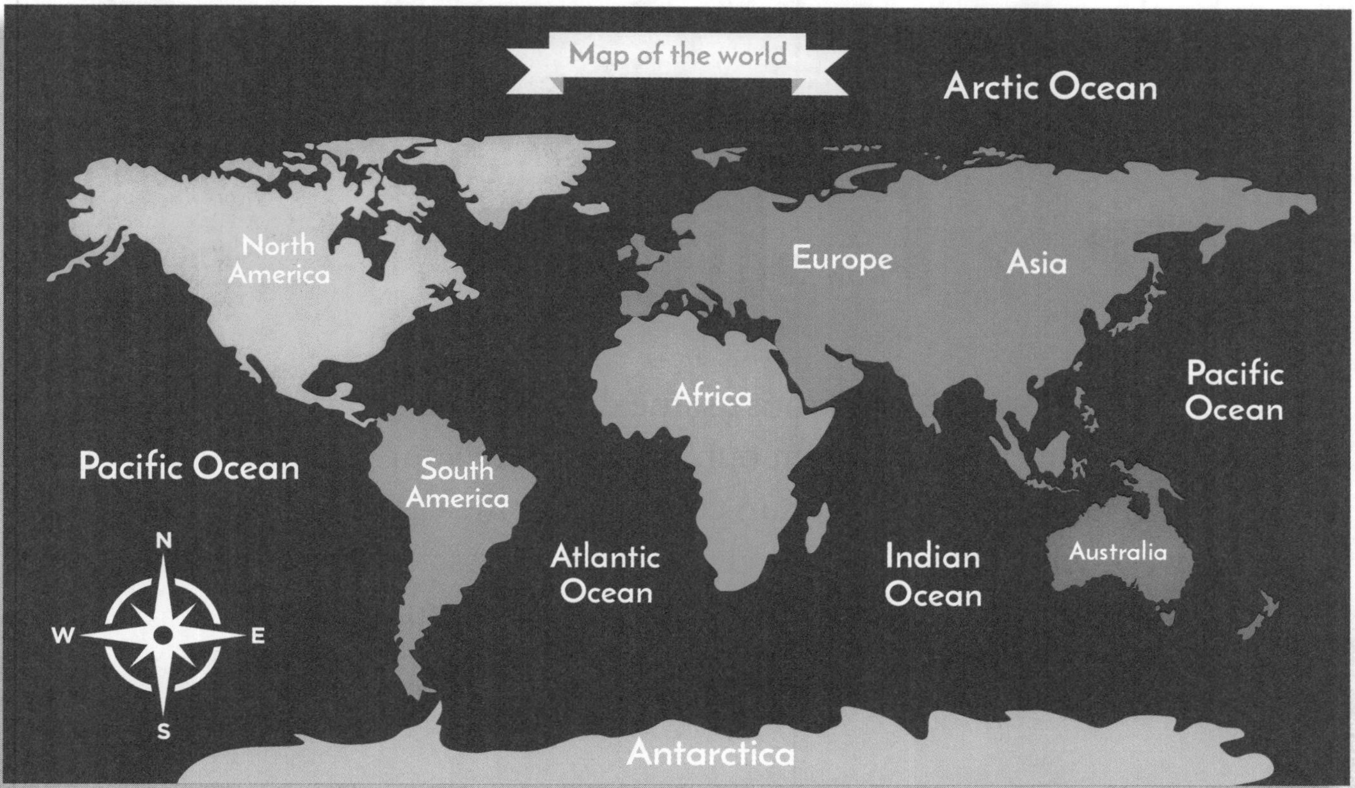

Take a look at the zoo! Imagine you are there and are currently with your family in the middle of the zoo. If you wanted to go to the elephant, there to the right, which direction would you need to go? Make sure you check the compass direction key! If you wanted to see the camel instead, there to the left, which direction would you need to go? If you preferred to see the monkey, which direction would you need to go? If you preferred to go to the entrance of the zoo, which direction would you need to go?

If you go outside, you can find those same directions in a fairly simple way. Just stand and put your hands straight out, making sure your right hand is pointing to where the sun comes up. The sun comes up in the east, so your left hand is pointing west, which is where the sun goes down. As you stand like this, you are actually looking north, and your back is to the south. Try it!

Get your God's Scripture Time flashcards ready! We are talking about **maps** in this lesson, and this verse helps us know that wherever we go in the world, God will be there with us. Now listen to this one again, then say it with me:

> *Fear not, for I am with you . . .* (Isaiah 43:5).

Help the fox and rabbit find their way to their house through the city maze below. Please note that you should never actually let a rabbit drive your car!

↑ Finish

Start →

Language 07:00 time!

Some people in the world speak a language called Lithuanian. If you want to say "thank you" in Lithuanian, you just say *achiu* (ah choo). Let's say it now, kindly: *achiu*. There are people in a country called Lithuania who speak this language. Why don't you get your continent map of Europe and color in Lithuania!

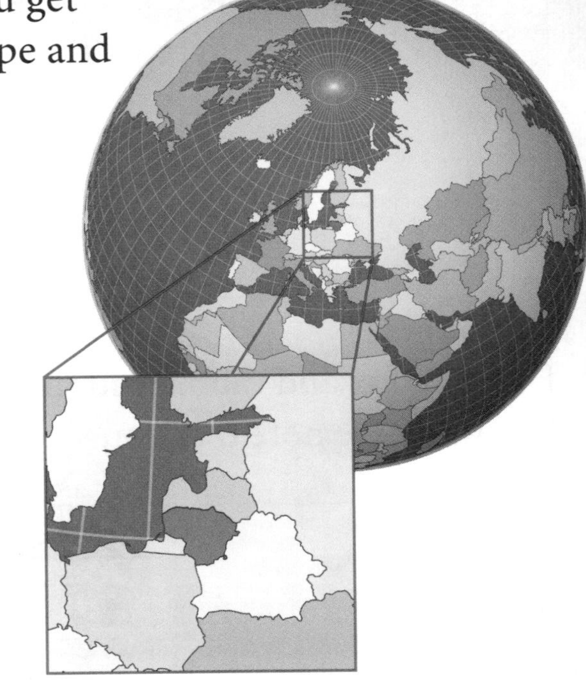

Name

Picture time!

Color the image of a boy and a world map below.

You are growing up in a time when many people don't look at printed **maps** anymore. Many **maps** are viewed on phones now! But there is still a need to create visual ways to look at the world so we can travel safely when we drive to places we've never been or at least places we don't know very well. To help us do this, there are mapmakers who keep printed **maps** up to date with new or changed roads, as well as programmers who make **maps** interactive on phones and other devices so they can help us as we're driving.

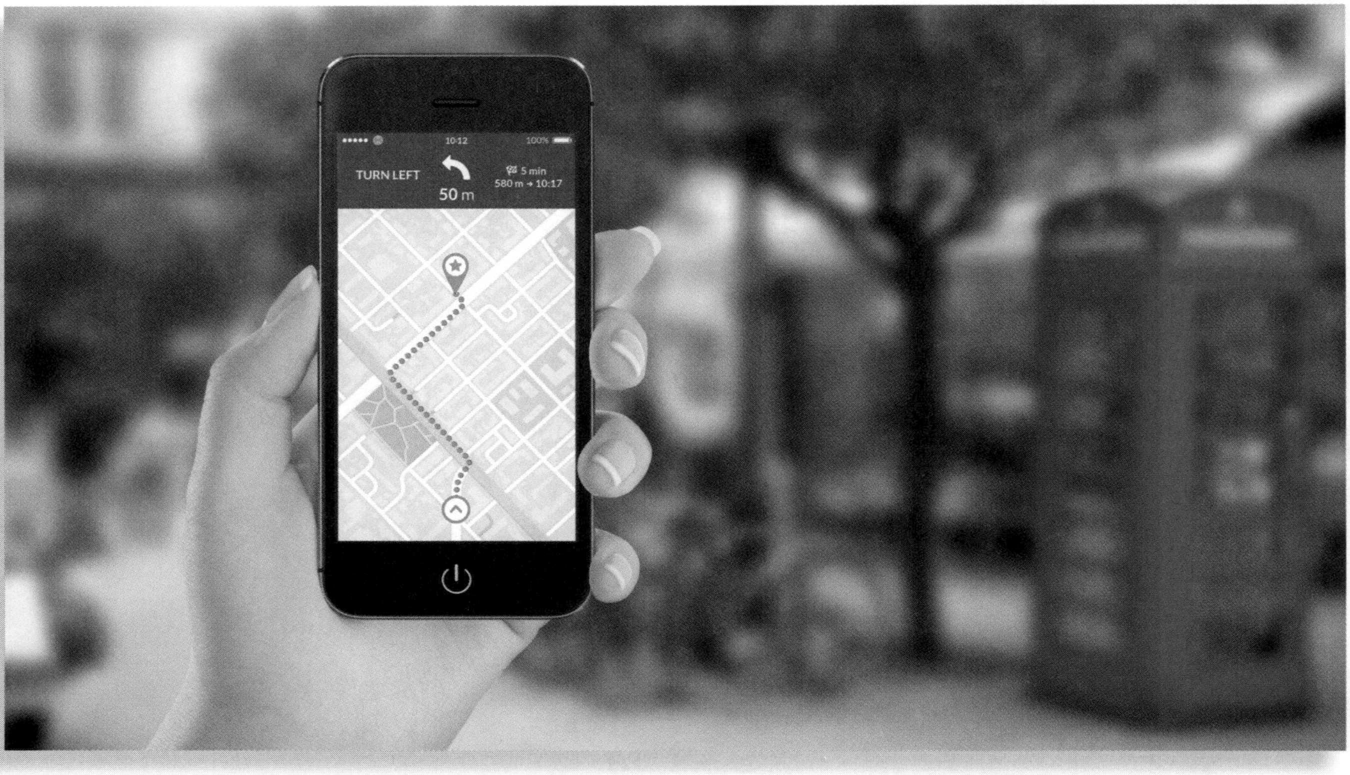

There are so many different kinds of **maps** you can find! Have you ever tried to follow a map that would guide you and your family through a store or a park? Does your family travel with a GPS map to guide them?

Turn to the Lesson 20 My Book Time page in the back of this book to complete your story for the week in words and colors!

A Metro to My World

Community

LESSON #21

TEACHER NOTES

Developmental Mile Markers

Languages: Learning a new language is easiest for children prior to age 8. The brain is most open to language reception during these early years. In nearly every community, there are people who speak other languages and have different cultural backgrounds. Learning another language can help us connect to people in a way they best understand and connect God's love to others.

SUPPLIES

- ☐ Crayons or colored pens or pencils

Lesson Goals

Students should be able to:

- Discuss the foundation of a good community and how people come together to make their part of the world better.

word collector **Community**: A group of people who live and work close together.

Name

Let's smile into the new week because it's go time!

Wherever you live, around you there is a **community** of other people who live near you. A good **community** is a group of people who live and work close together, who often have similar things they like or don't like, and who often help and support each other. A church is a special **community** of people who love God, who try to love others like Jesus would, who believe the teachings of the Bible, and who care for those in need. It is so good to go through life with people around you who care for you and who you care for as well. Everyone has special strengths and gifts they bring to their **community** that help make their part of the world so much better.

God's Scripture time

Get your God's Scripture Time flashcards ready! We are talking about **community** in this lesson, and this verse helps us know that a part of being a blessing to our **community** is being kind, having a tender heart, and forgiving each other.

Now listen to this one again, then say it with me:

And be kind to one another, tenderhearted, forgiving one another, even as God in Christ forgave you (Ephesians 4:32).

Language time!

Some people in the world speak a language called Mandarin. If you want to say "thank you" in Mandarin, you just say *xiexie* (shay shay). Let's say it now, in an excited way: *xiexie*. There are people in a country called China who speak this language. Why don't you get your continent map of Asia and color in China!

Name ______________________________

Picture time!

Seek and Find. Find the following community places in the picture, then color them in.

Cafe Bank Church

The word ***community*** can mean "people sharing a close space," like a town, or it can mean "people who share similar beliefs and ideas." Either way, there are people who help our communities grow stronger and sweeter every day. These **community** helpers include voting registration workers who help us make sure we can vote and make our voices heard, veterinarians who take care of our pets to make sure they stay healthy, manicurists who keep our toenails and fingernails clean and well groomed, and hair stylists who cut and style our hair.

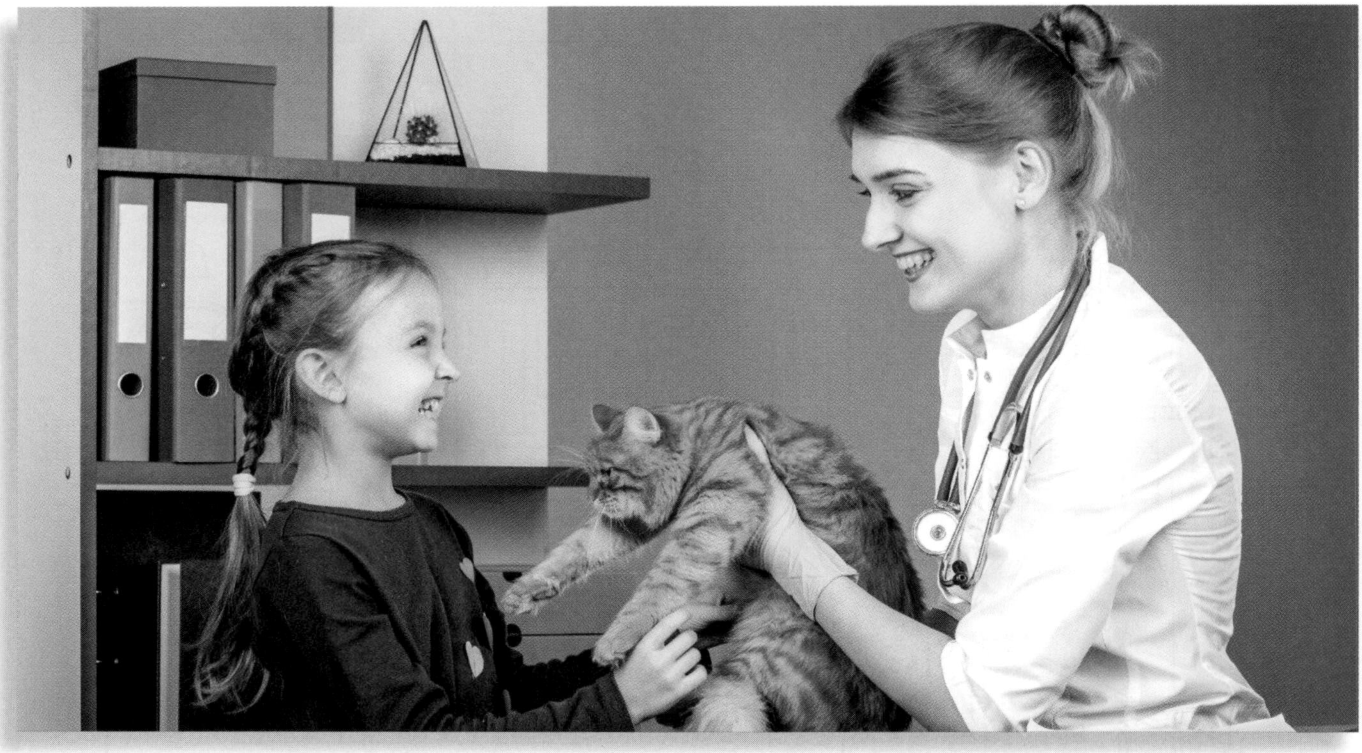

Community is such a wonderful word to describe a place where people can be connected to each other and happy together. What are some of your favorite things that come to mind when you think about your **community** and the people you know there?

Turn to the Lesson 21 My Book Time page in the back of this book to complete your story for the week in words and colors!

A Helicopter Flight with Everything in Sight

Rural and Urban Worlds

LESSON #22

TEACHER NOTES

Developmental Mile Markers

Gross Motor Skills: Children 4 to 5 years old should be able to hop on one foot, throw a ball overhand, and balance on each foot. These are skills that can be developed in either rural or urban worlds quite easily.

Lesson Goals

Students should be able to:

- Compare and contrast rural communities with urban communities and show the value of each.

SUPPLIES

- ☐ Crayons or colored pens or pencils
- ☐ Scissors
- ☐ Glue or tape

Rural: A word that means out in the country, not in the city.

Name

Let's get in the helicopter. It's go time!

We have talked about city life and country life a little already. Well, ***rural*** is a word that means in the country, and *urban* is a word that means in the city. Both have much to make them wonderful.

Usually, urban life has more people closer together, has more jobs and shopping places, and has access to more hospitals and banks. City life can be very busy and loud. Usually, **rural** life has less people in a close area, has fewer possible jobs and places to shop, and has less access to hospitals and banks. Country life can be a little less busied and a little quieter.

There are people in the city and people in the country who love God and love others, and they know that where you live is a choice you make, so try to make others around you feel loved and supported no matter where you live.

Cut out the buildings and backgrounds, then glue or tape each building to its proper background.

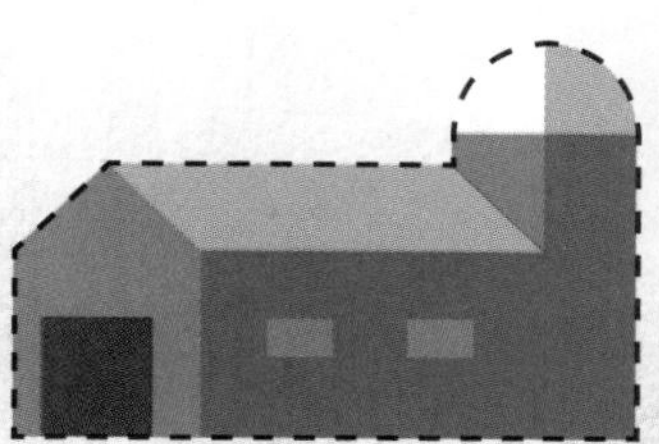

Get your God's Scripture Time flashcards ready! We are talking about **rural** and urban communities in this lesson, and this verse helps us know that whether we live in the city or the country, God made us so wondrously, and we can find joy in praising Him. Now listen to this one again, then say it with me:

> *I will praise You, for I am fearfully and wonderfully made; marvelous are Your works, and that my soul knows very well* (Psalm 139:14).

Language 07:00 time!

Some people in the world speak a language called Norwegian. If you want to say "thank you" in Norwegian, you just say *takk* (talk). Let's say it now, in a happy way: *takk*. There are people in a country called Norway who speak this language. Why don't you get your continent map of Europe and color in Norway!

Name

MY STORY K
Lesson 22
Exercise 2 Day 2

Picture time!

Is this a picture of a farm or a city? Is this a picture of urban life or rural life? Circle your answers.

 Farm City	 Farm City
 Urban Life Rural Life	 Urban Life Rural Life

We know that **rural** means "in the country" and urban means "in the city." There are helpers in both those areas that make life better for us. If you live out in the country, you might know ranchers who work hard to raise cattle, shepherds who work hard to raise sheep, or refinery workers who work hard to process oil and other fuels. If you live in the city, you might know retail workers who work hard to keep things we need ready for us in stores, restaurant workers who work hard to provide meals for us, or mechanics who work hard to keep our cars running well.

Whether you live on a farm or ranch, in a big city, or somewhere in between, home is a beautiful place to be! How would you describe your home and the surrounding area to someone who had never been there?

Turn to the Lesson 22 My Book Time page in the back of this book to complete your story for the week in words and colors!

Yachts and Yachts of Folks

Different People of the World

LESSON #23

TEACHER NOTES

Developmental Mile Markers

The Developing Brain: The brain of a child goes through so much change in the first 3 to 7 years of life; it is actually 90 percent developed by age 5. Vision and hearing are developing, then language, then higher cognitive functions. Parents are vital to helping provide a positive, loving environment so children grow in the healthiest way. The brain is most flexible when children are young, and this is the same for children all over the world.

SUPPLIES

- ☐ Crayons or colored pens or pencils

Lesson Goals

Students should be able to:

- Recognize that people around the world have certain similarities and differences and that God loves all of us and wants us to love as He does.

Nationality: Who you are because of the country where you were born.

Name

Go time!

There are so many wonderful people in the world. That's right, it's go time!

What country do you live in? Did your family always live there, or did some people from your family long ago come from other countries? The nation you are from reflects your **nationality**, but this is only one part of what makes you *you*.

Now, the more people you read about or meet from around the world, the more you will find there is much we all share. All people in the world seek to love and be loved, to share special times with others, and to enjoy good food. And though every country has a somewhat different history, God loves all of us from every country or **nationality** and desires all of us to know Him and to find salvation in Jesus.

So even if someone wears clothing that looks a little different than yours, or speaks a different language than yours, or eats something a little different than what you like to eat, deep down we long to live in peace with our families and friends.

God's Scripture time

Get your God's Scripture Time flashcards ready! We are talking about different people in the world in this lesson, and this verse helps us to keep our focus on the Lord and His goodness no matter whom we might be with and to love them like God loves us. Now listen to this one again, then say it with me:

Rejoice in the Lord always. Again I will say, rejoice! (Philippians 4:4).

Language time!

07:00

Some people in the world speak a language called Oriya. If you want to say "thank you" in Oriya, you just say *dhanyabahd* (dun ya bawd). Let's say it now, in a surprised way: *dhanyabahd*. There are people in a country called Thailand who speak this language. Why don't you get your continent map of Asia and color in Thailand!

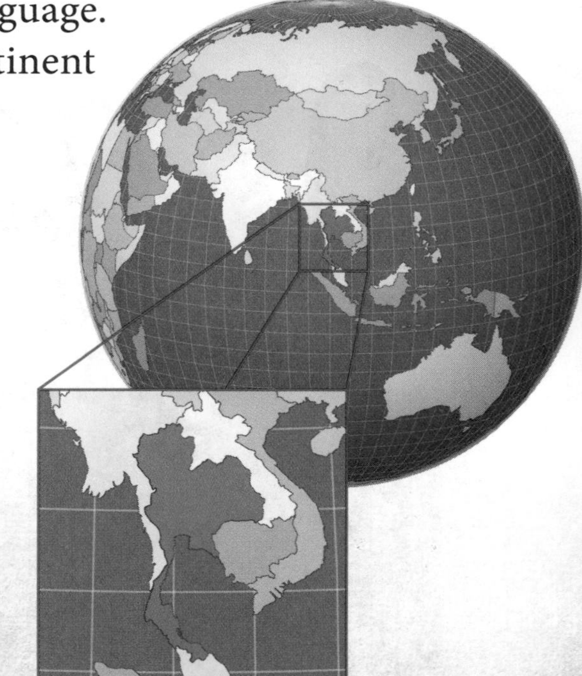

Name

Picture time!

Spring Holidays and Festivals Around the World: The Festival of Colors is in March and is celebrated by people in India just after the wheat harvest. Mother's Day is celebrated in March in England, and May in the United States, honoring the love and lives of mothers. Easter is celebrated by Christians around the world in March or April, honoring the death and Resurrection of Jesus, God's only Son.

The Great Passion Play, Eureka Springs, Arkansas

Color the picture of the mouse helping harvest wheat.

Did you know there are almost 8 billion people in the world? That's a lot of people! In some ways, we are all very similar, and in some ways, we are very different, depending on where in the world we are born. But there are a lot of community helpers who try to keep us connected. Pilots and flight attendants help fly us to different places in the world so we can work with others and make friends with others. Museum workers help us understand history and cultures so we can appreciate our differences more. And language translators help us know what other people are saying if they are speaking one of the over 7,000 languages in the world we might not understand.

God made so much wonder in His world, with so many wonderful people for us to know and love. What do you think are some of the best things about us all being just a little different? What things about us are very much alike?

Turn to the Lesson 23 My Book Time page in the back of this book to complete your story for the week in words and colors!

A Taxi Is Nice, Takes Me Everywhere Twice

Different Parts of the World

LESSON #24

TEACHER NOTES

Developmental Mile Markers

Storytellers: By the time children finish kindergarten, many will be able to tell stories, expressing thoughts and feelings with their words. Children all over the world learn stories and learn to share their stories with others. These stories often help teach moral principles and good versus bad character.

SUPPLIES

- ☐ Crayons or colored pens or pencils

Lesson Goals

Students should be able to:

- Explain the way we understand the world across countries and time zones.

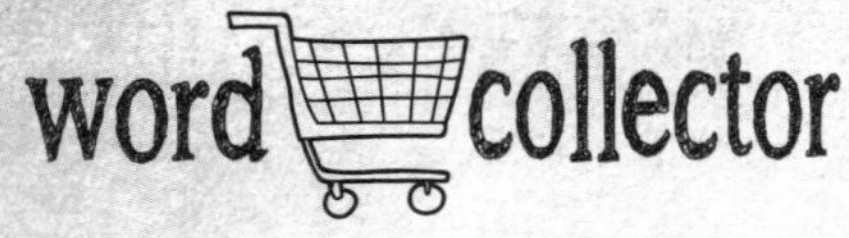

word collector **Time zones**: The earth is divided into 24 areas, or zones, where time is different.

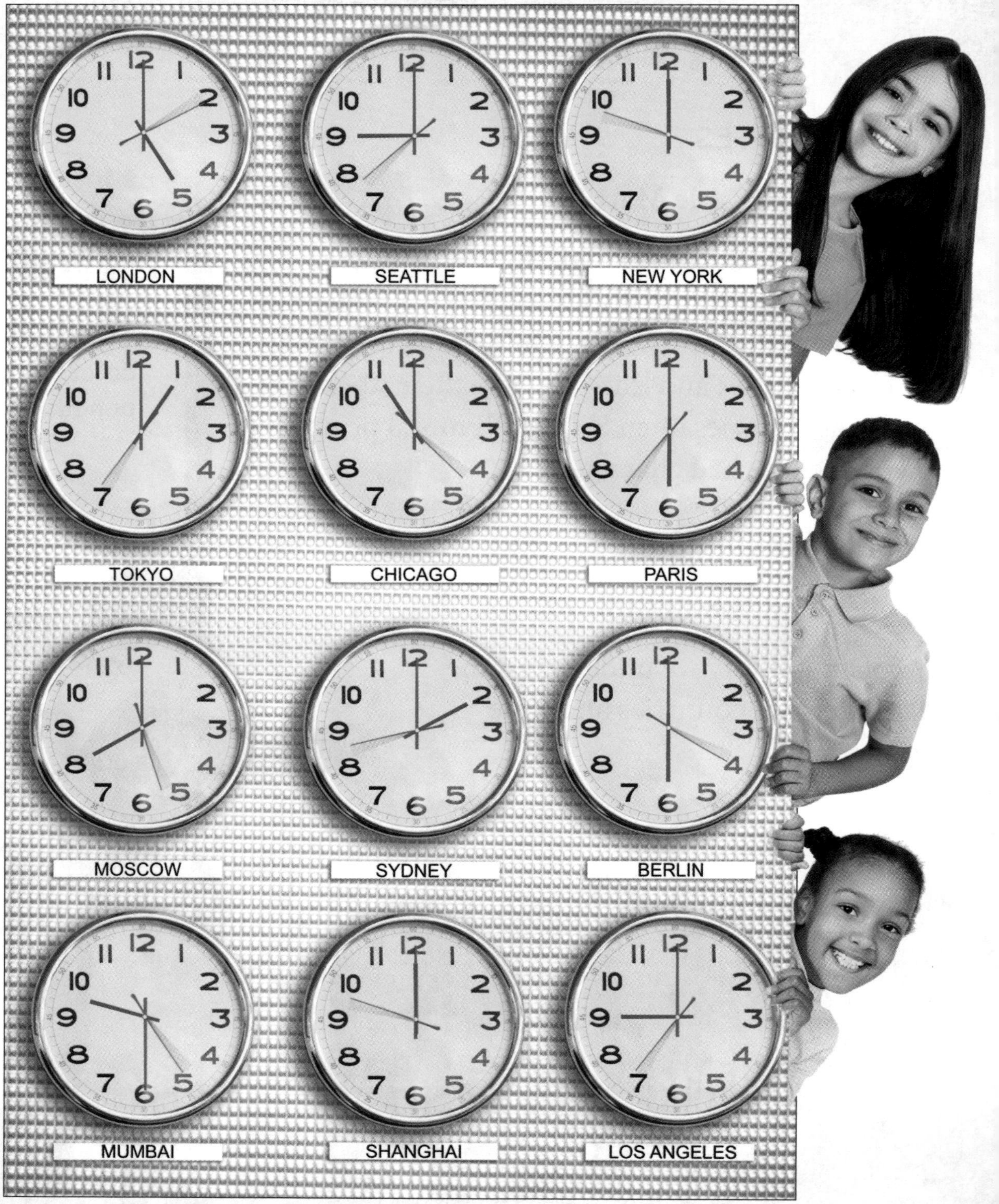
LONDON
SEATTLE
NEW YORK
TOKYO
CHICAGO
PARIS
MOSCOW
SYDNEY
BERLIN
MUMBAI
SHANGHAI
LOS ANGELES

Name

MY STORY K
Lesson 24
Exercise 1 Day 1

We're going to explore this week because it's go time!

We each live in a place we call home, and it is in the city or countryside, and that place is in a state or province, and all of that is a part of the country you live in and the continent you live on. And because God's world is so big, people have divided the earth into 24 **time zones**. It might be 3 o'clock in the afternoon at your house, and midnight where someone else lives! Have your teacher show you where your country is on the map. (See world map on the back.)

You can know that if you are looking out your window at sunrise, some people have already enjoyed the morning and are eating lunch, some people are having dinner at sunset, and some people are asleep in the middle of the night. Yes, the world is that big!

Get your God's Scripture Time flashcards ready! We are talking about different parts of the world in this lesson, and this verse helps us remember to love our neighbors, no matter where in the world we might be, because a neighbor is simply someone we can help. Now listen to this one again, then say it with me:

You shall love your neighbor as yourself (Matthew 22:39).

Some people in the world speak a language called Pashto. If you want to say "thank you" in Pashto, you just say *tashakor* (tash ah koor). Let's say it now, in a tired way: *tashakor*. There are people in a country called Pakistan who speak this language. Why don't you get your continent map of Asia and color in Pakistan!

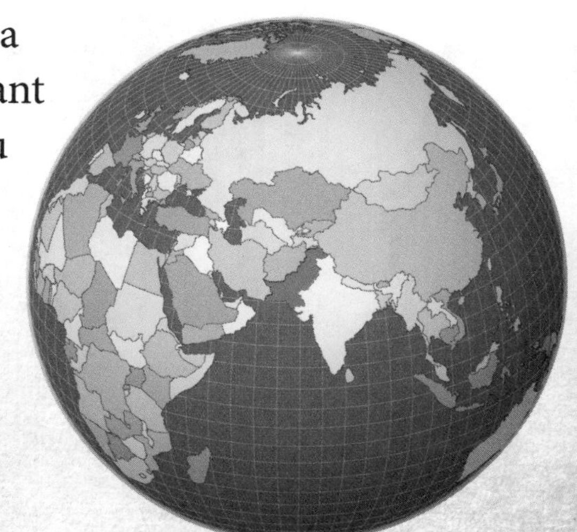

Have your teacher help you find your time zone and maybe a few other places you know!

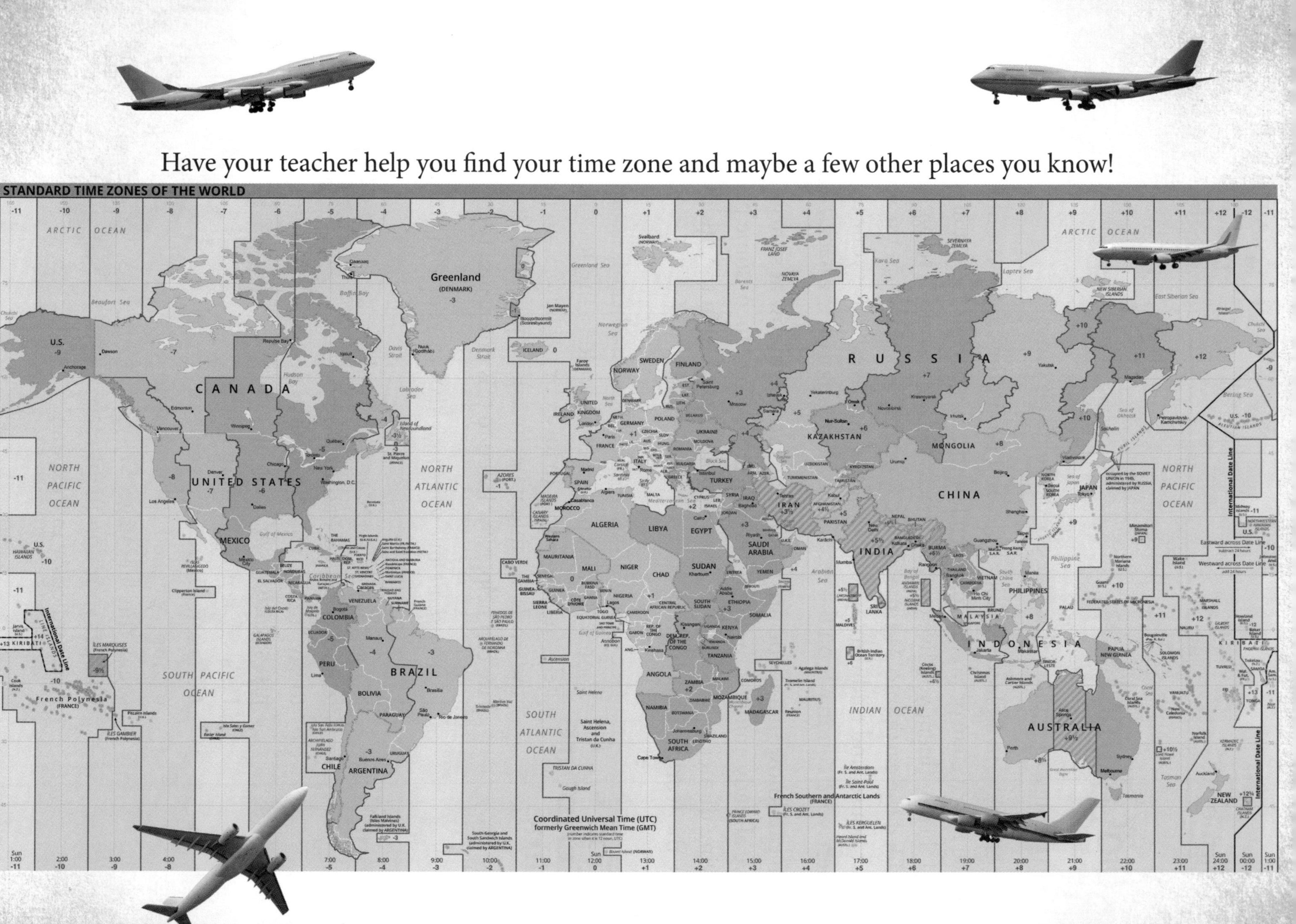

Name ________________________________

Picture time!

Circle whether you do this in the morning, the afternoon, the evening, or the night.

Morning 

Afternoon Evening

Afternoon Evening

Morning Night

Helping hands time!

Just as there are many people in the world, there are also many countries where people live too. In fact, there are almost 200 different countries in the world, covering the 24 **time zones**, each with various mountains, lakes, deserts, and more. To help us explore these wonderful landscapes, you will want to connect with local helpers, including park rangers who can tell you about state or federal parklands, fish and game wardens who make sure wildlife is cared for, and researchers who study the land so we can protect it for future generations.

Talk time!

There are so many countries in the world with so much to see in them. Is there a country you would like to visit one day? What is something about your country that amazes you?

My Book time!

Turn to the Lesson 24 My Book Time page in the back of this book to complete your story for the week in words and colors!

Trolley Bound with Food All Around

What the World Eats

LESSON #25

TEACHER NOTES

Developmental Mile Markers

Healthy Choices: You can help children make healthy choices by having them help out with a family garden or help in meal preparation. It can also be interesting to see what kinds of foods are eaten around the world, some being just what your family eats and some things you might never have thought to eat!

SUPPLIES

☐ Scissors

Lesson Goals

Students should be able to:

- Explain that people around the world eat many things that we do and some things we might never eat.

Food: What we eat to give us energy and keep us strong.

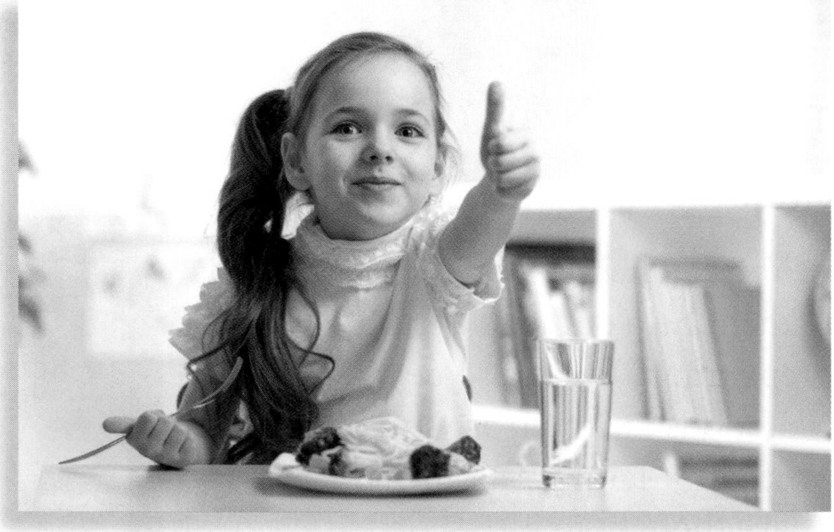

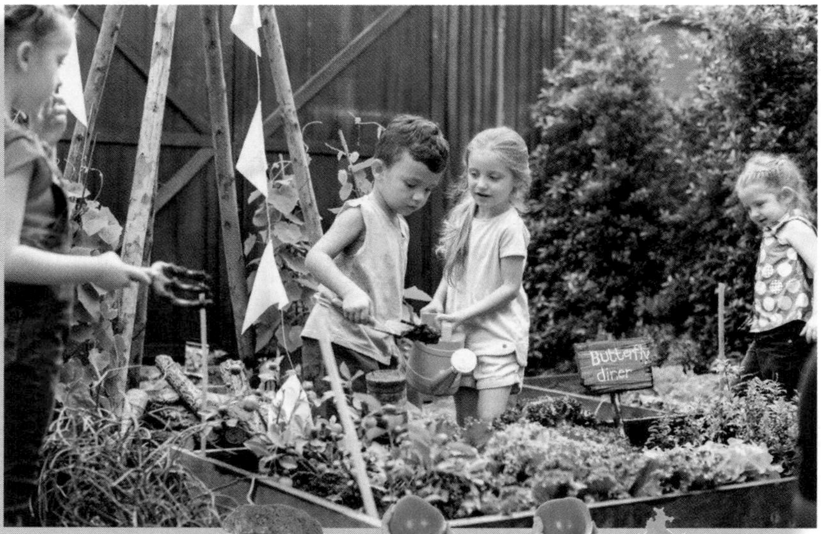

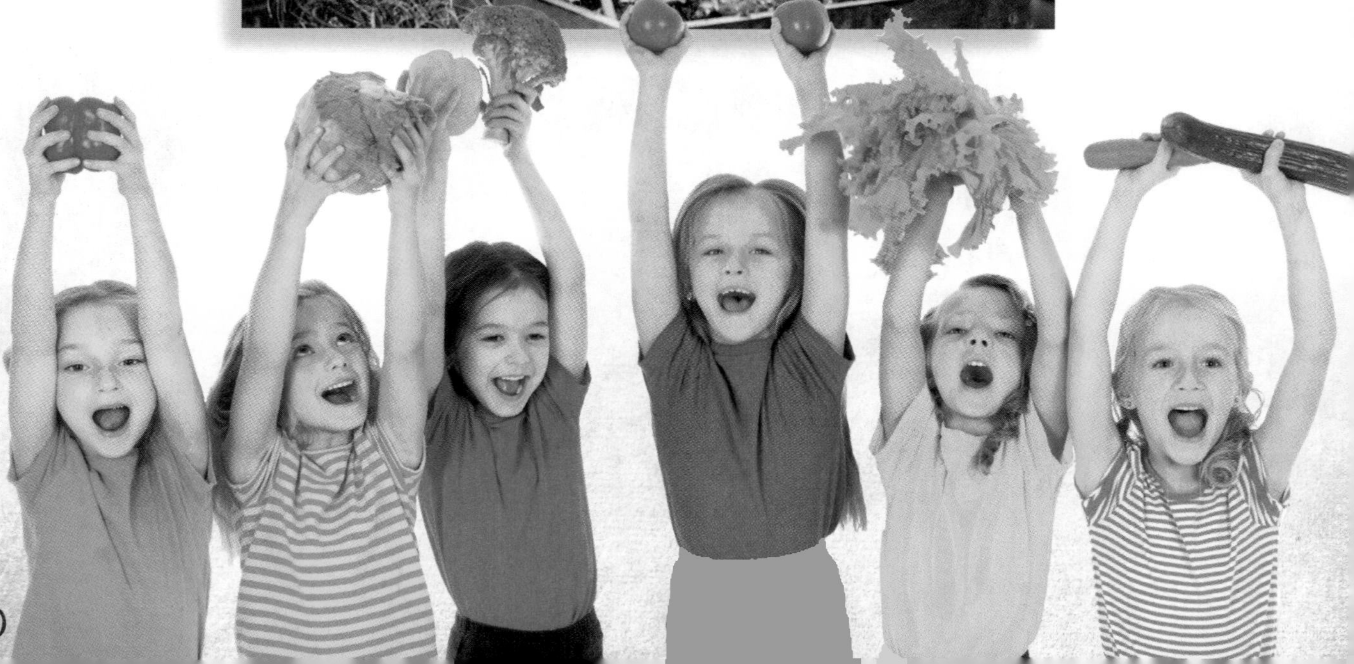

Name

Go time!

This week is all about **food**, so I hope you're hungry. It's go time!

You probably already knew that everyone in the world eats **food**, but we don't all eat the exact same **food**. See if you recognize some of these foods from around the world:

- If you live in a country called Bosnia-Herzegovina, you might eat jufka, zvijezda ghee, or hot dogs.
- If you live in a country called Kuwait, you might eat macaroni, lamb, or dates.

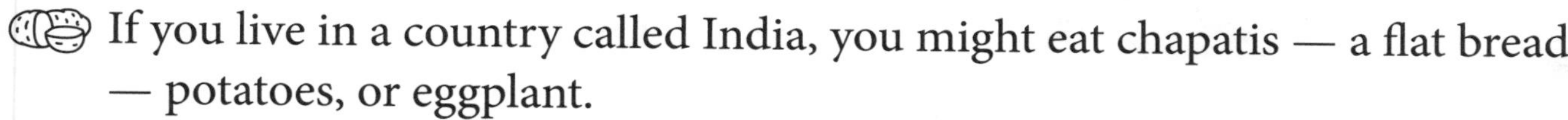

- If you live in a country called India, you might eat chapatis — a flat bread — potatoes, or eggplant.
- If you live in a country called the Philippines, you might eat green mandarin oranges, kangkong spinach, or bitter gourd.
- If you live in a country called Japan, you might eat octopus, clams, or bacon.
- If you live in a country called Chad, you might eat dried fish, goat meat, or okra.
- If you live in a country called China, you might eat rice balls (above), pigs' feet, firedrake fruit, or eel strips.
- If you live in a country called Guatemala, you might eat chayote squash, chicken, or inti pasta.
- If you live in a country called Ecuador, you might eat plantains, lentils, or carrots.
- If you live in a country called France, you might eat grenadier fish, duck, or artichokes.

If you live in a country called Greenland, you might make a stew from seal meat and rice.

In some countries, you can buy **food** from street vendors that include sea horses, cicadas, hot pretzels, pig intestines, and cotton candy.

How many of those foods did you know?

Get your God's Scripture Time flashcards ready! We are talking about what the world eats in this lesson, and this verse helps us remember that we love God by keeping His commandments, which are not hard on us. One simple way we can show God's love is by providing food to people in need — directly, through our church, or through a local food pantry. Now listen to this one again, then say it with me:

For this is the love of God, that we keep His commandments. And His commandments are not burdensome (1 John 5:3).

Language 07:00 time!

Some people in the world speak a language called Quechua. If you want to say "thank you" in Quechua, you just say *yusulpayki* (yoo sool pie key). Let's say it now, in a friendly way: *yusulpayki*. There are people in a country called Bolivia who speak this language. Why don't you get your continent map of South America and color in Bolivia!

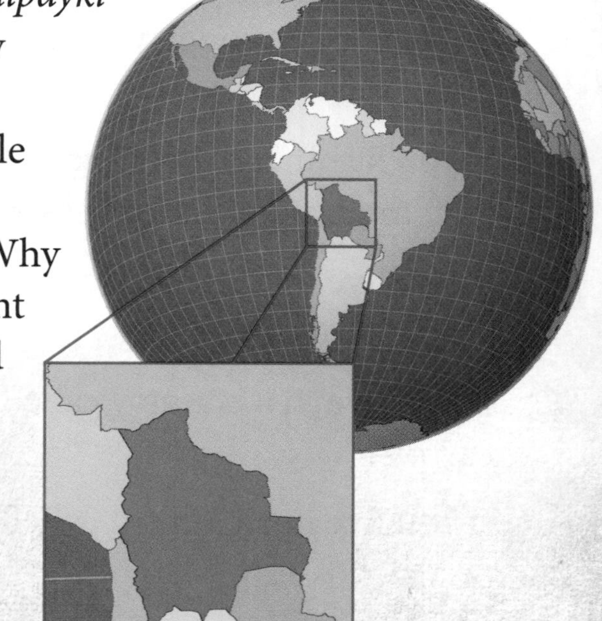

Name

MY STORY K
Lesson 25
Exercise 2 Day 2

Picture time!

Cut out the different kinds of foods and build a delicious meal on your plate. Consider laminating the page before you cut.

Page blank for cutting purposes.

Helping hands time!

In every community, there are people who help make sure we have everything we need to eat and drink well. This would include people who get our **food** to us, like those who work in local farmer's markets and who deliver **food** directly to our homes. It would also include those who sell us appliances like refrigerators to keep our **food** cold and ovens to cooks our **food**, as well as those who provide us with water purifiers to make sure our water is healthy to drink.

From burritos to bugs, people around the world eat lots of amazing things! What are some of your favorite things to eat? Do you prefer sweet things, salty things, sour things, or a little bit of everything?

Turn to the Lesson 25 My Book Time page in the back of this book to complete your story for the week in words and colors!

Seaplane Wings and Geographic Things

Geography Terms

LESSON #26

TEACHER NOTES

Developmental Mile Markers

Healthy Reading Habits: Time for reading each day to young children has many wonderful benefits. This time can help the child think of reading as a joyful practice, improve his or her attention span, show them that reading is something important, help a child's vocabulary, and lead to a strong self-esteem.

SUPPLIES

- ☐ Crayons or colored pens or pencils
- ☐ Scissors
- ☐ Geography Flashcards

Lesson Goals

Students should be able to:

- Describe various aspects of the world, including mountains, rivers, and oceans.

word collector **Geography**: A word that means writing about the earth.

Name

MY STORY K
Lesson 26
Exercise 1 Day 1

Keep soaring on seaplane wings this week. Come on, it's go time!

Geography is a word that means writing about the earth. Now would be a good time to pull out the **Geography** Flashcards from the back of the book. Read through the descriptions about lakes, rivers, mountains, and more to be able to match them with the pictures on the other side of the flashcard.

Did you recognize all the **geography** terms? Were there any you just learned? What is a term that describes somewhere you have been? What is a term that describes where you would like to go?

God's Scripture time

Get your God's Scripture Time flashcards ready! We are talking about **geography** terms in this lesson, and this verse helps us remember that as we learn and live, we should trust in the Lord's wisdom and not our own, no matter where we might be on His wondrous earth. He can help you know what is good and right. Now listen to this one again, then say it with me:

Trust in the Lord with all your heart, and lean not on your own understanding . . . (Proverbs 3:5).

Language time!

Some people in the world speak a language called Russian. If you want to say "thank you" in Russian, you just say *spasibo* (spy see bow). Let's say it now, in a neighborly way: *spasibo*. There are people in a country called Russia who speak this language. Why don't you get your continent maps of Europe and Asia and color in Russia! It's big!

Name ______________________

Picture time!

Where is my home? Draw a line from the animal to the home or habitat it is missing from.

Geography involves knowing about the earth, and there are people in communities around the world who help us do just that. And you might grow up to be one of these helpers one day, including geologists who study land and rocks, paleontologists who study life that was trapped in fossils during the Flood of Noah, volcanologists who study volcanoes, and seismologists who study earthquakes. Pretty amazing helpers!

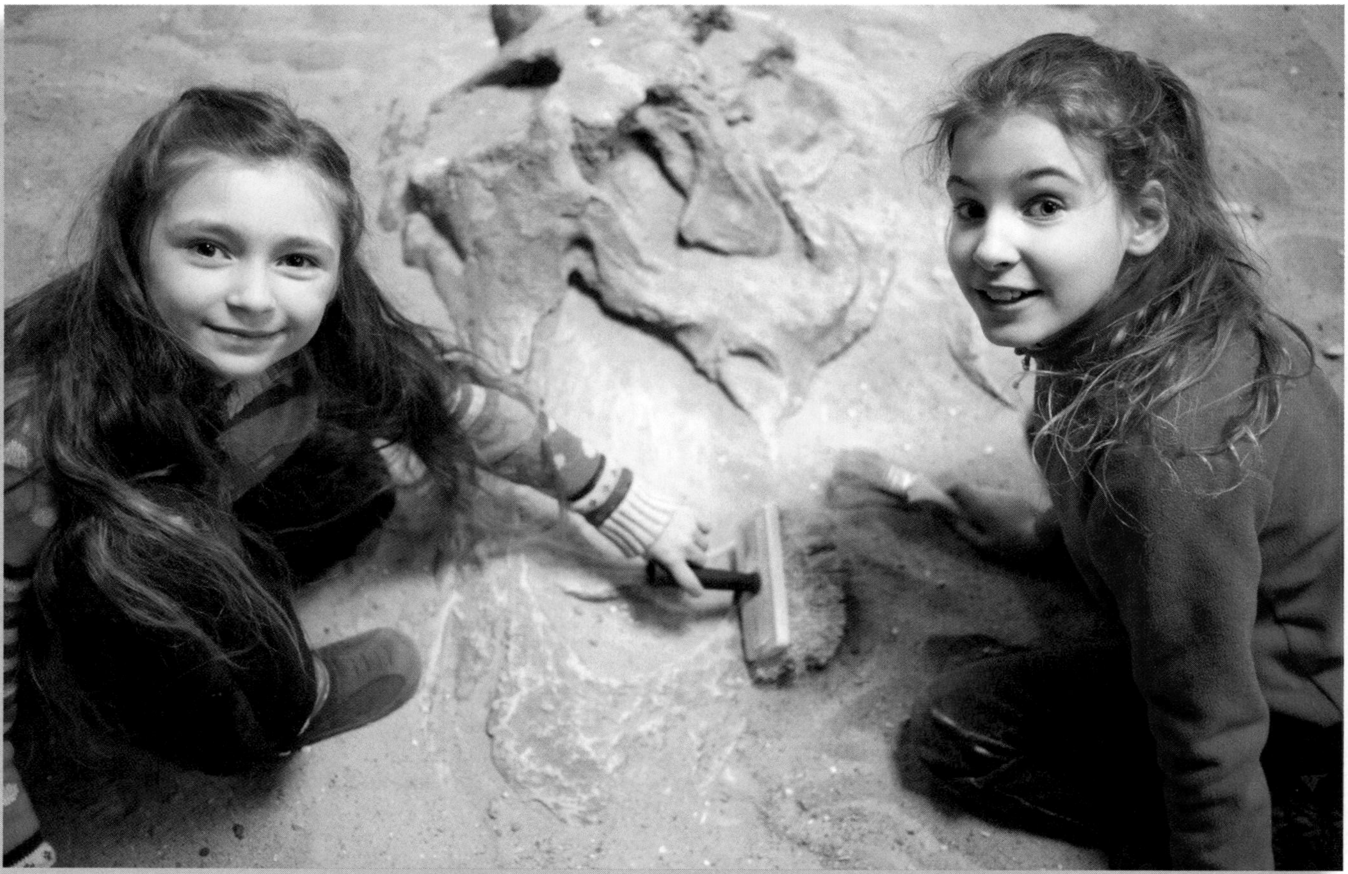

Mountains, valleys, and deserts . . . oh my! What is your favorite place of God's creation to go to with your family?

Turn to the Lesson 26 My Book Time page in the back of this book to complete your story for the week in words and colors!

Subways and Seasons

Weather Words

LESSON #27

TEACHER NOTES

End of week recipe ingredients:

- ☐ 4 yams, skinned and sliced into thick pieces (sweet potatoes can also be used)
- ☐ 1 cup brown sugar, divided
- ☐ 2 cinnamon sticks, divided
- ☐ 4 tablespoons butter or margarine, divided
- ☐ Salt, to taste

SUPPLIES

- ☐ Crayons or colored pens or pencils
- ☐ Scissors
- ☐ Word Collector flashcards (for review)
- ☐ See recipe

Developmental Mile Markers Review

Healthy Activity: You can help children keep active by having them choose sports they like, keep active with your family, or find enjoyment in activity each day. And whether you live in the city or country, getting outside whenever you can helps keep you connected to God's wondrous creation.

Fine Motor Skills: Children 4 to 5 years old should be able to copy some shapes, use a spoon and fork, and use scissors to cut on lines. All these skills will help children discern the varied shapes and lines on maps so they can tell roads from rivers and more.

Languages: Learning a new language is easiest for children prior to age 8. The brain is most open to language reception during these early years. In nearly every community, there are people who speak other languages and have different cultural backgrounds. Learning another language can help us connect to people in a way they best understand and connect God's love to others.

Gross Motor Skills: Children 4 to 5 years old should be able to hop on one foot, throw a ball overhand, and balance on each foot. These are skills that can be developed in either rural or urban worlds quite easily.

The Developing Brain: The brain of a child goes through so much change in the first 3 to 7 years of life; it is actually 90 percent developed by age 5. Vision and hearing are developing, then language, then higher cognitive functions. Parents are vital to helping provide a positive, loving environment so children grow in the healthiest way. The brain is most flexible when children are young, and this is the same for children all over the world.

Storytellers: By the time children finish kindergarten, many will be able to tell stories, expressing thoughts and feelings with their words. Children all over the world learn stories and learn to share their stories with others. These stories often help teach moral principles and good versus bad character.

Healthy Choices: You can help children make healthy choices by having them help out with a family garden or help in meal preparation. It can also be interesting to see what kinds of foods are eaten around the world, some being just what your family eats and some things you might never have thought to eat!

Healthy Reading Habits: Time for reading each day to young children has many wonderful benefits. This time can help the child think of reading as a joyful practice, improve his or her attention span, show them that reading is something important, help a child's vocabulary, and lead to a strong self-esteem.

Lesson Goals

Students should be able to:

- Identify the meaning of words that describe the world's weather.

Weather: Different patterns of wind and water in the sky that make earth hot or cold.

Name

MY STORY K
Lesson 27
Exercise 1 Day 1

Go time!

We've already come to the end of another quest? Well, come on, it's go time!

You probably already know a little something about **weather**. Sometimes it's sunny, and sometimes it's rainy. Sometimes it's snowy, and sometimes it's really hot. And when it's summer in what is called the Northern Hemisphere, it's actually winter in the Southern Hemisphere.

There are many reasons why God created the world with such unique **weather** patterns. He makes sure mountains are covered in snow because when the snow melts, it feeds rivers and lakes, and this water also flows into the oceans. Rains can bring life to forests and farms. Deserts have their own unique life that God created to grow there. Winds come to help carry seeds so they can grow wild.

Get your God's Scripture Time flashcards ready! We are talking about **weather** words in this lesson, and this verse helps us remember that the most important thing is to believe in Jesus and to love. It shouldn't matter if it is sunny or stormy, our faith or belief in Jesus shouldn't change, and we should always be found loving others. Now listen to this one again, then say it with me:

And this is His commandment: that we should believe on the name of His Son Jesus Christ and love one another, as He gave us commandment (1 John 3:23).

Language time!

Some people in the world speak a language called Serbian. If you want to say "thank you" in Serbian, you just say *hvala* (hvah lah). Let's say it now, in a polite way: *hvala*. There are people in a country called Serbia who speak this language. Why don't you get your continent map of Europe and color in Serbia!

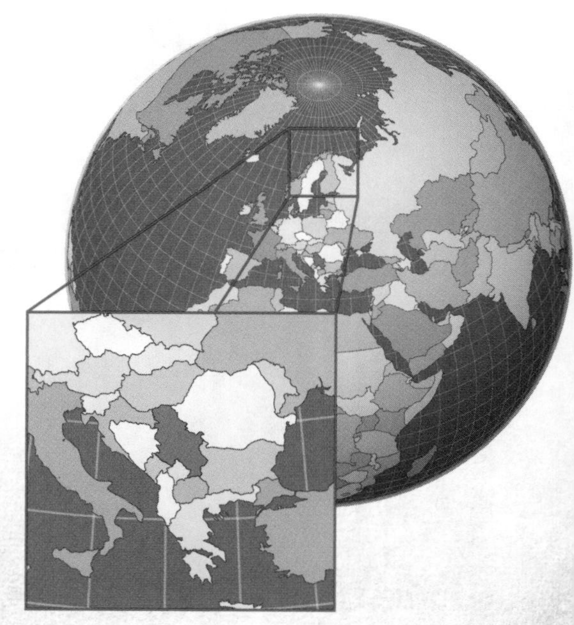

Name ______________________________

Draw a line between the matching word and picture.

clouds

sun

rain

snow

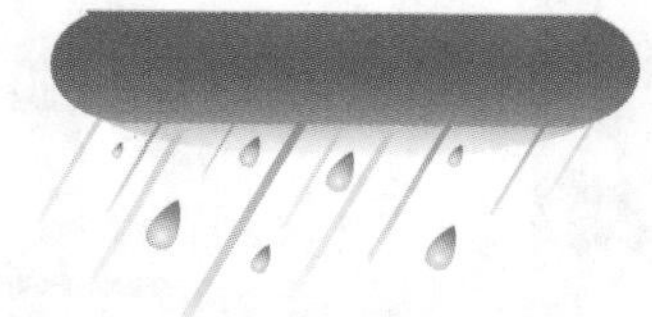

lightning

rainbow

Because **weather** patterns can change fairly quickly, watching and knowing the **weather** can be very important for us. For example, if you want to play in the park, but it's going to storm, you might need to change your plans. There are helpers in our communities that tell us what to expect and whether we might see storms or sunny skies in the next few hours or days. Air traffic controllers help guide planes into airports safely and have to watch wind patterns, meteorologists let us know about **weather** patterns so we can know if rain or snow might be expected, and wind turbine technicians monitor areas where it is most windy so wind turbines can generate power for us.

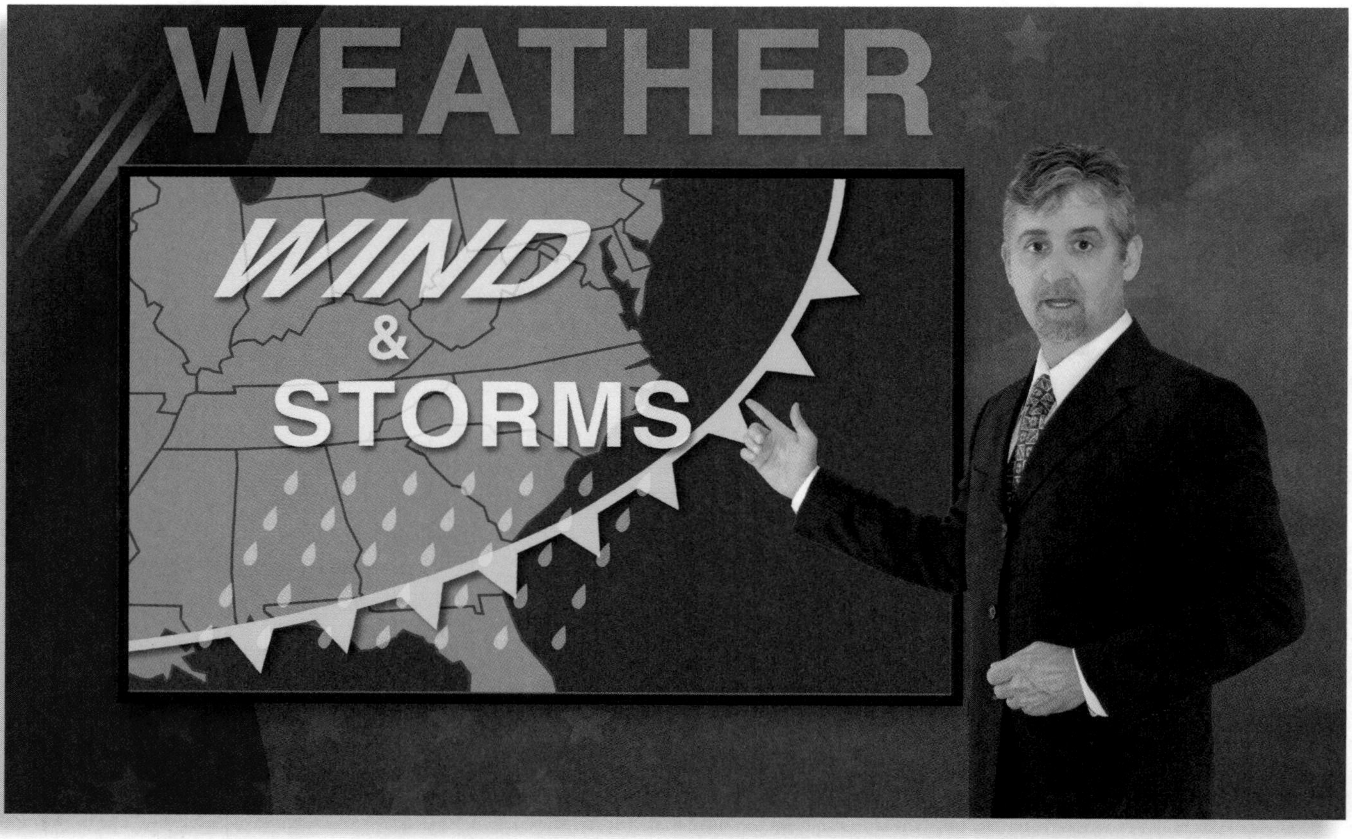

Sometimes it rains, or snows, or sometimes it's sunny, but whether it's windy or still or stormy and loud, what is your favorite kind of **weather**? Why is it your favorite?

Turn to the Lesson 27 My Book Time page in the back of this book to complete your story for the week in words and colors!

Vegetables Around the World!

Vegetables are the part of a plant that are edible or able to be eaten. The part of the plant that we eat depends on the particular plant. The leaves of lettuce, spinach, and kale are the part we eat. For radishes, carrots, beets, and parsnips, we eat the roots of the plant that grow underground. Tubers are also grown underground and are considered starch vegetables. Examples are potatoes, cassava, yams, sweet potatoes, taro, Jerusalem artichokes, jicama, and ginger. There are many different types of vegetables. What's listed here is only a small sample. All vegetables are an important part of a healthy diet, providing vitamins and nutrients that are needed for us to grow.

What types of vegetables do you like? Do you like your vegetables raw, cooked, or both? What type of vegetables do you have in your refrigerator or pantry or cupboard? If you have a farmer's market or fresh foods market in your area, go on a visit and see which different kinds of vegetables you can find. Try a new vegetable and see what you think.

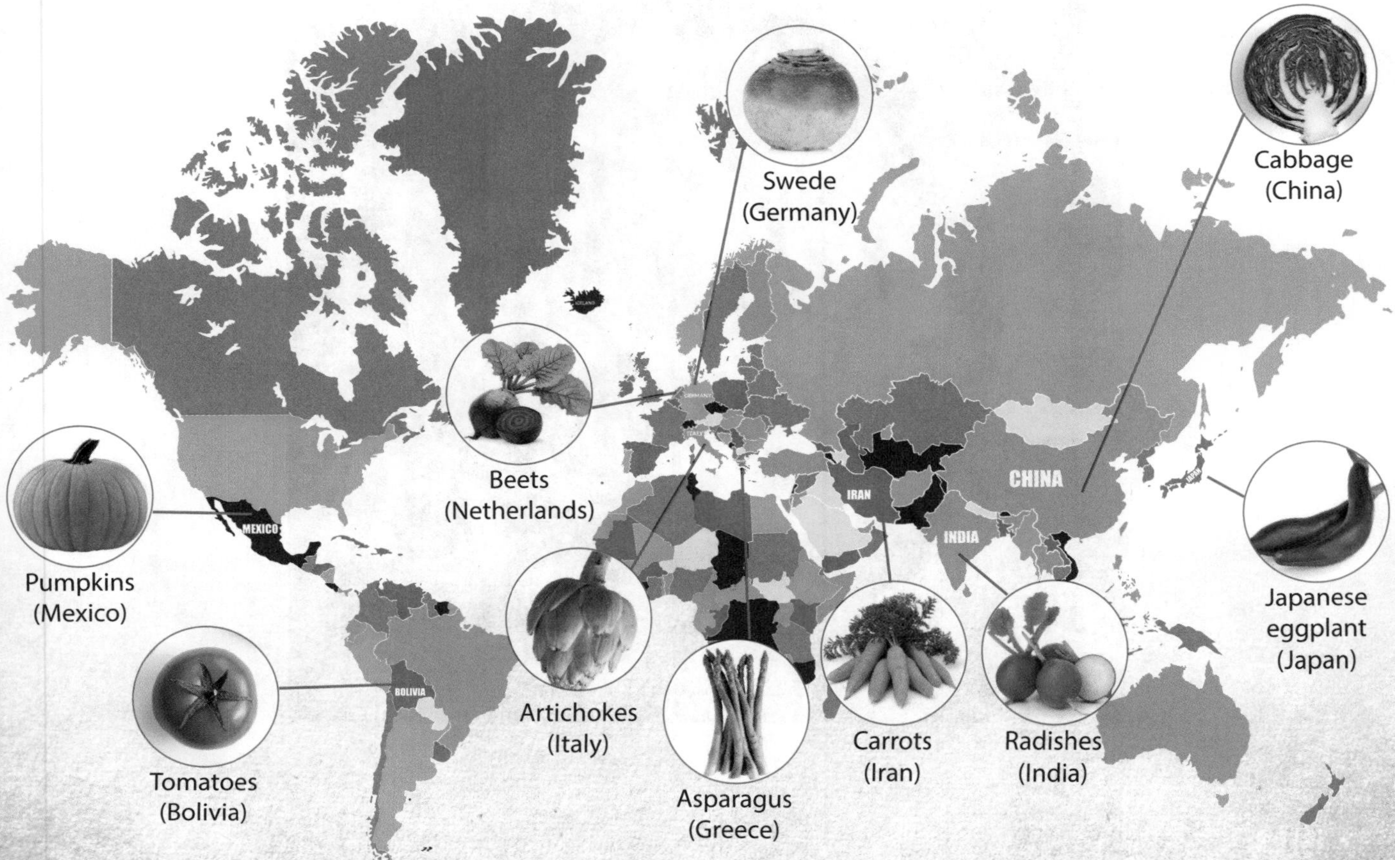

Swede (Germany)

Cabbage (China)

Beets (Netherlands)

CHINA

IRAN

INDIA

MEXICO

BOLIVIA

Pumpkins (Mexico)

Japanese eggplant (Japan)

Tomatoes (Bolivia)

Artichokes (Italy)

Asparagus (Greece)

Carrots (Iran)

Radishes (India)

Here's a recipe to try and make with your teacher:

Yams

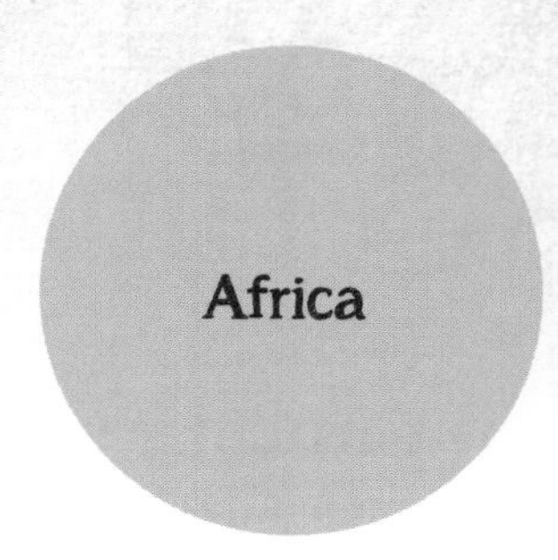

Ingredients

- ☐ 4 yams, skinned and sliced into thick pieces (sweet potatoes can also be used)
- ☐ 1 cup brown sugar, divided
- ☐ 2 cinnamon sticks, divided
- ☐ 4 tablespoons butter or margarine, divided
- ☐ Salt, to taste

In a heavy pan or Dutch oven, layer each ingredient beginning with the butter, yams, sugar, salt, and cinnamon sticks. Repeat layers. No water is needed. Place lid on pot and cook over low heat for about 2 ½ hours and yams are tender.

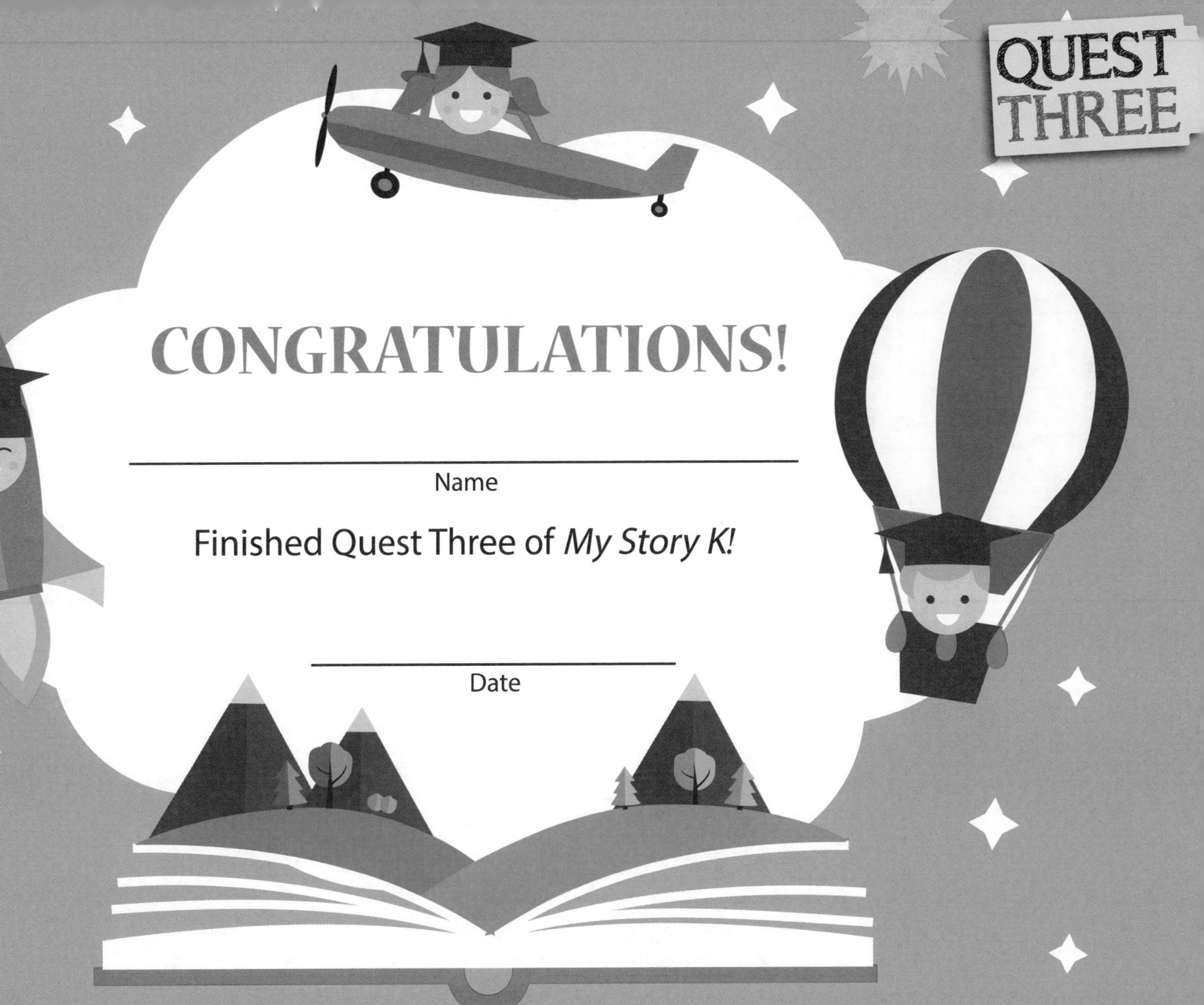
QUEST THREE
CONGRATULATIONS!
Name
Finished Quest Three of *My Story K!*
Date

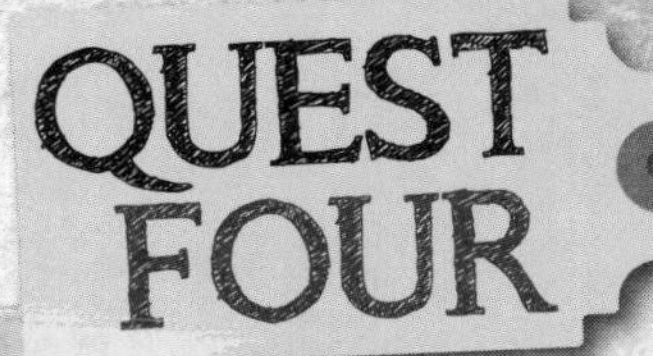

Quest Collector Card!

Tear out this page and circle the bolded words as you find them in the lessons!

1. A **need** is something necessary or important for you.
2. **Wants** are things we would like to have, but we don't have to have them to be healthy or safe.
3. In all parts of the world, **money** in the form of coins or paper can be traded for goods and services.
4. Psalm 139:14 says, "I will **praise** You, for I am fearfully and wonderfully made; marvelous are Your works, and that my soul knows very well."
5. Philippians 4:4 says, "Rejoice in the **Lord** always. Again I will say, rejoice!"
6. Things that can be **recycled** include some cans, paper, plastic, and cardboard.
7. Goods are products you can buy (like books), while **services** are not things you can touch, but things people do for you (like medical care).
8. In all you do now and in all you will do one day, you can **trust** in the Lord completely, and He will give you the wisdom and knowledge you need.
9. No matter what you end up doing in your **life**, you should believe in Jesus and should love others.

Follow the Language Time countries on the map from Lessons 28–36

On a Gondola of Goods

What a Family Needs

LESSON #28

TEACHER NOTES

Developmental Mile Markers

Choices: As children grow older, give them more choices to help them mature in making decisions. This might include choosing what to wear, what games to play, or what to have as a snack. It will eventually help them learn to distinguish between the value of needs and wants.

SUPPLIES

- ☐ Crayons or colored pens or pencils

Lesson Goals

Students should be able to:

- Describe what families need in order to feel peace and to be healthy and safe.

word collector **Needs**: These are things we must have that we can't do without.

Name

Go time!

It's time for the last quest to begin. You know what that means: it's go time!

There are many things that families need to make sure they are healthy and safe. A **need** is something necessary or important for you. A **need** is a thing we really can't do without, including water to drink, food to eat, and a home or shelter. Jesus spoke of God caring for our needs so that we don't sit around and worry about what He will provide for us. He also gives us the strength to work when we get older so we can earn our living and provide for our families as best as possible.

Each week for this fourth and last quest, you will be going back over the Bible verses you learned in the first quest and showing how well you know them. We are talking about finances in this fourth quest, and this verse helps us know that Christ gives us all we **need** to provide for us today and in every tomorrow. Now listen to this one last time, then say it with me:

I can do all things through Christ who strengthens me (Philippians 4:13).

Language 07:00 time!

Some people in the world speak a language called Slovak. If you want to say "thank you" in Slovak, you just say *dakujem* (jah koo yehm). Let's say it now, in a cool way: *dakujem*. There are people in a country called Slovakia who speak this language. Why don't you get your continent map of Europe and color in Slovakia!

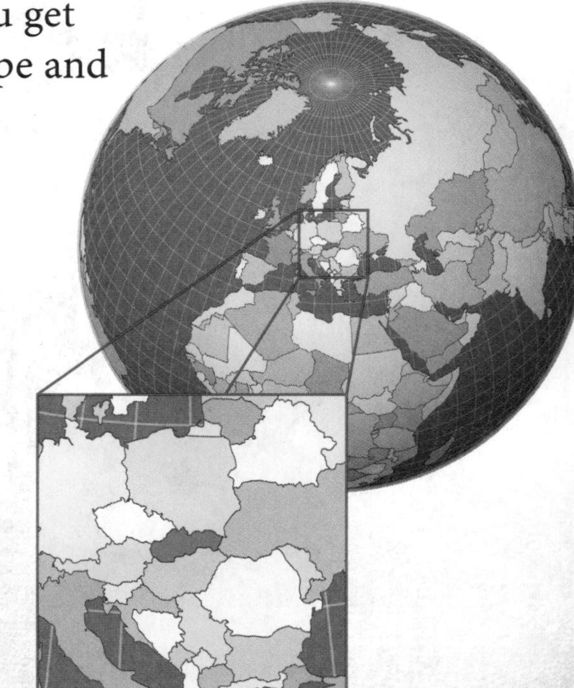

Name

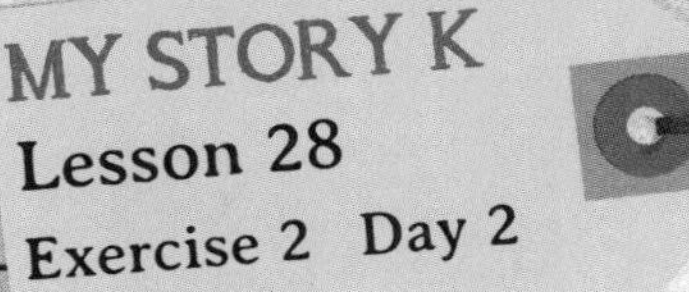

Picture time!

Got Pizza? Color the right number of pizza slices so that the kids pictured can each have one slice.

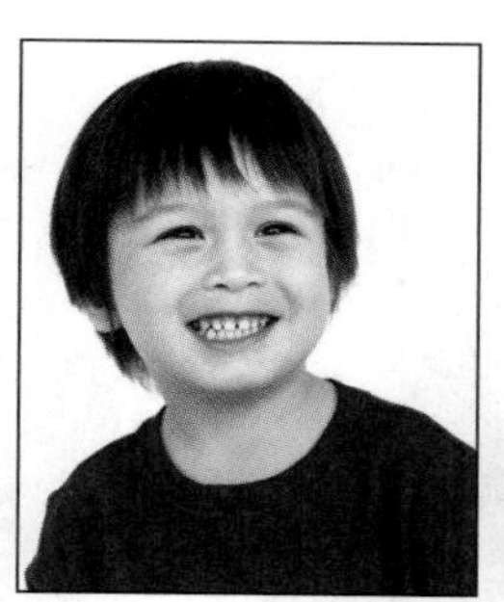

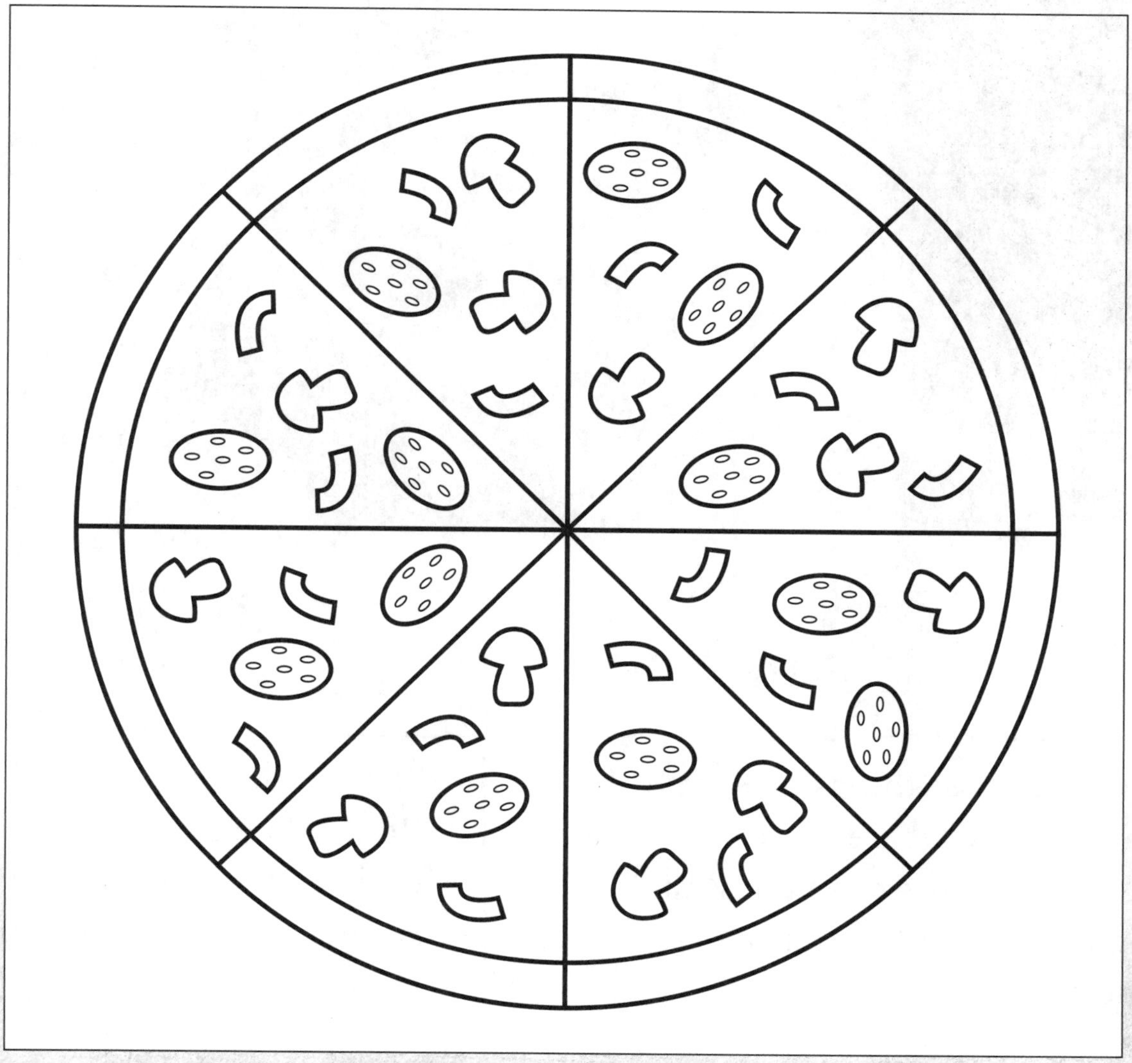

Families around the world all have some similar needs to fill to help them be healthy and safe. And in our communities, there are men and women who step up to fill these needs for us. We all **need** to get our teeth checked and repaired when they get cavities, so hygienists and dentists help us with these things. Because we **need** insurance to help pay for our medical costs , there are people who help us get everything we **need**. And because we **need** homes to live in, construction workers are so important to have in our communities.

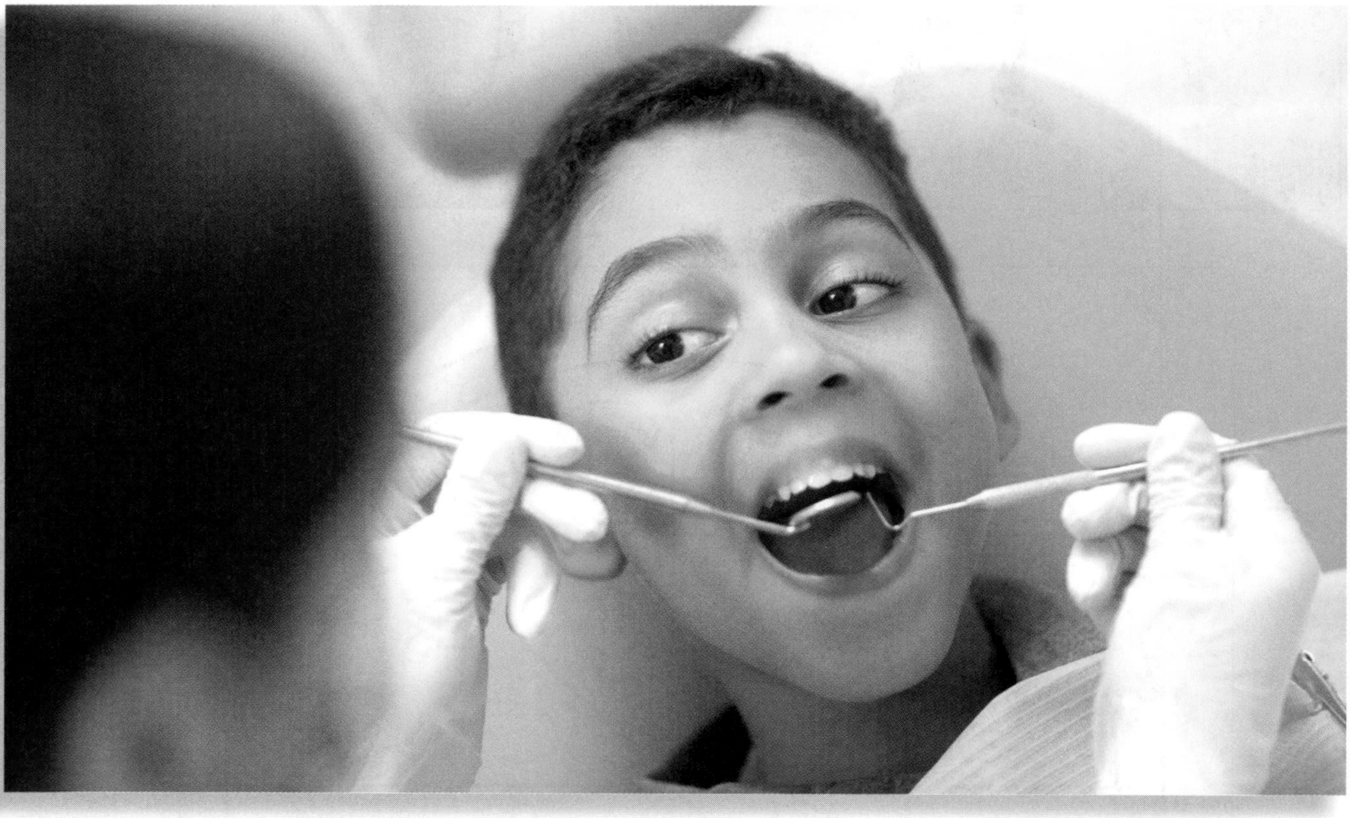

Needs are those things we simply must have. What are some of the most important needs your family has? Would your whole family agree on those needs?

Turn to the Lesson 28 My Book Time page in the back of this book to complete your story for the week in words and colors!

On a Bobsled of Bounty

Needs Versus Wants

LESSON #29

TEACHER NOTES

Developmental Mile Markers

Solving Problems: If your child becomes upset about a situation, make sure to help him or her work through simple problem-solving steps if there is anything he or she might do to help makes things better. Just as we learn to choose between what is most needed and what is simply a want, we also learn that our responses to situations are also ours to choose.

SUPPLIES

- ☐ Crayons or colored pens or pencils

Lesson Goals

Students should be able to:

- Compare and contrast needs versus wants.

word collector **Wants**: These are things we would like to have but can live without.

Name

There's so much to learn this week. That must mean it's go time!

Last week you heard about needs, things important or essential for us. **Wants** are things we would like to have, but we don't have to have them to be healthy or safe. Circle the things you think are needs and tell your teacher why. It's nice to have a few things we want that we don't have to have.

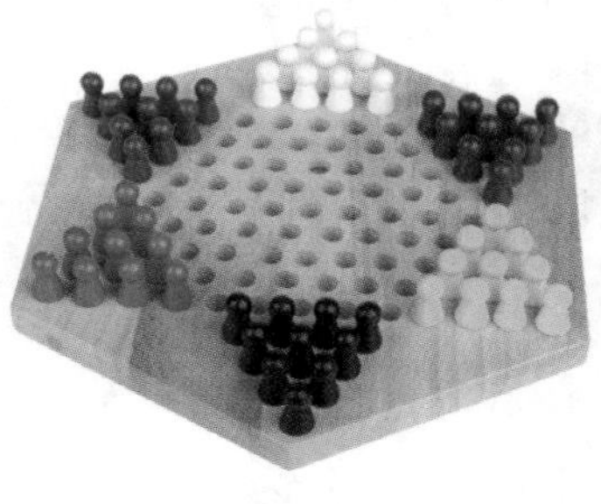

God's Scripture time

Get your God's Scripture Time flashcards ready! We are talking about needs versus **wants** in this lesson, and this verse helps us know that God will be with us everywhere we go, and when He's with us, we don't need to fear not having what we really need. Now listen to this one last time, then say it with me:

Fear not, for I am with you . . . (Isaiah 43:5).

Language 07:00 time!

Some people in the world speak a language called Spanish. If you want to say "thank you" in Spanish, you just say *gracias* (graw see us). Let's say it now, in a warm way: *gracias*. There are people in a country called Mexico who speak this language. Why don't you get your continent map of North America and color in Mexico!

Name

Picture time!

Sammy the Pig always wanted a tricycle. He finally got one. Color the image below of Sammy riding his trike.

Just as needs are things we really must have, **wants** are things we would love to have if we could. They are good but not quite as important. People that meet some of the **wants** in our community are coffee shop workers who provide coffees and lattes, ice cream shop workers who provide delicious ice cream in a cone or bowl, mini golf workers who let us have fun playing mini golf, and bowling alley attendants who let us have a good time bowling.

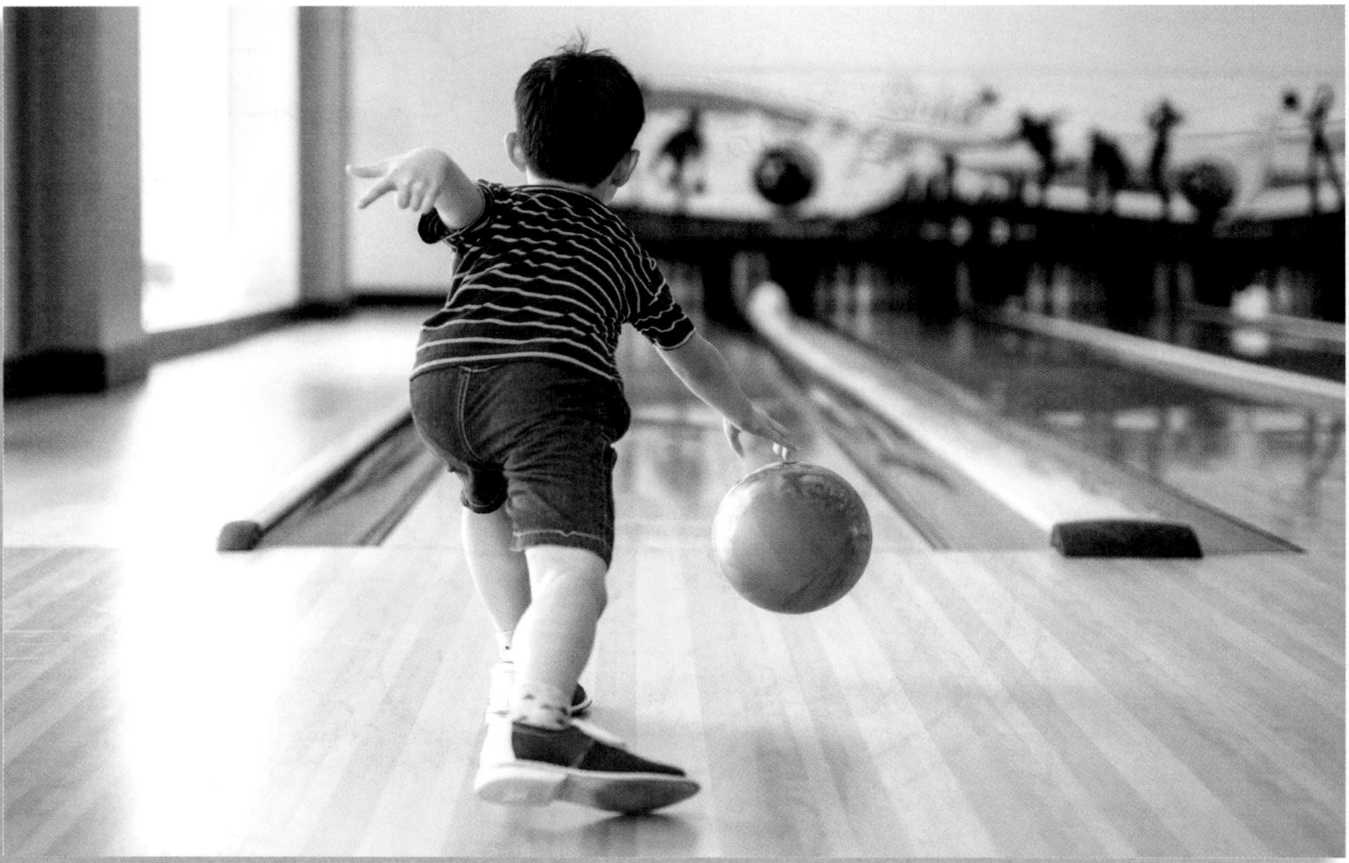

Now, needs are those things we simply must have, and **wants** are those things we would really like to have. What are a few needs and **wants** you and your family need and want?

Turn to the Lesson 29 My Book Time page in the back of this book to complete your story for the week in words and colors!

On a Kayak with Cash

Trade, Borrow, or Purchase

LESSON #30

TEACHER NOTES

Developmental Mile Markers

Self-worth: Parents and teachers can help young children develop their esteem by giving praise for things they accomplish, encouraging them to do new things, establishing realistic goals, and by not being overly critical to them. One way this can be fostered is through simple, age-appropriate work around the house, possibly getting an allowance for work done well, and then guiding the children to save or spend responsibly.

SUPPLIES

- ☐ Crayons or colored pens or pencils
- ☐ Some coins

Lesson Goals

Students should be able to:

- Describe the different ways we can get the things we need or want.

word collector **Purchase**: To buy things from a person or a store.

Name ____________________

Hop in your kayak because it's go time!

In all parts of the world, money in the form of coins or paper can be traded for goods and services. You can go to stores, markets, or even garage sales to **purchase** things you like.

There are other ways to get some of the things you need and want as well. You might have a friend who has something you like, and he or she doesn't really want it anymore. And maybe you have something your friend would like that you don't really want anymore. In this case, you could trade the two items so you both have something you want. Trade is how most things were paid for hundreds of years ago.

One last way to get something you might want is through something called borrowing. You don't really own something you borrow, and you have to give it back when you're done. That's how it works at the library when you check out a book or DVD.

God's Scripture time

Get your God's Scripture Time flashcards ready! We are talking about trading or buying things in this lesson, and this verse helps us know that in all we do and say, and in all we buy or sell, we can show God's kindness and forgiveness.

Now listen to this one last time, then say it with me:

And be kind to one another, tenderhearted, forgiving one another, even as God in Christ forgave you (Ephesians 4:32).

Language 07:00 time!

Some people in the world speak a language called Turkish. If you want to say "thank you" in Turkish, you just say *tesekkur ederim* (te shay kooreh dur um). Let's say it now in a whisper: *tesekkur ederim*. There are people in a country called Turkey who speak this language. Why don't you get your continent map of Asia and color in Turkey!

Name

Picture time!

Sorting Coins. Gather some pennies, nickels, dimes, and quarters, or any mix of coins you might have in your home. In the United States, pennies are worth 1 cent, nickels are worth 5 cents, dimes are worth 10 cents, and quarters are worth 25 cents. How much are coins worth in the country you are from? Now, touch each coin to get a feel for each type, then put them all in a bowl. Have your teacher blindfold you, and then reach in and pull out one coin at a time, trying to guess which type of coin it is to sort them into like piles. Say the name of the coin as you put it in the pile.

U.S. Coins

Helping hands time!

Most often when we want or need something, we have to buy it with the money we have saved. However, sometimes we can get things with the help of others. If you want a car or need a house, you might speak with a loan officer at a bank in order to borrow the money you need. Also, you might go to someone holding a garage sale or to a consignment shop to buy used things or possibly to trade things for what you want. Sometimes friends even trade with us to help us out!

Talk time!

There are a lot of ways to get things that we like. You might trade with a friend one thing for another, borrow something from a family member to give back later, or buy something from a store with money you saved up. Can you think of one thing you've traded, one thing you've borrowed, and one thing you made a **purchase** of?

My Book time!

Turn to the Lesson 30 My Book Time page in the back of this book to complete your story for the week in words and colors!

So Much to See in a Blimp with Me

Choices

LESSON #31

TEACHER NOTES

Developmental Mile Markers

Healthy Emotions: You can help children develop healthy emotional responses by understanding that they may act out until they learn to control their emotions, listening to their worries and fears, and letting them speak about their emotions without putting them down. Ultimately, we all choose our response to situations, and God can give us the grace and peace to choose wisely.

Lesson Goals

Students should be able to:

- Identify ways to know we are making good choices.

SUPPLIES

- ☐ Crayons or colored pens or pencils

word collector **Choices**: Picking between two or more things that we want or need.

Name

Go time!

We're making so many **choices**. It must be go time!

Choose this or that. Every day you make **choices**, and the older you get, the more **choices** you'll make. Sometimes it starts with picking out what you are going to wear for the day, then maybe what you would like to eat. Perhaps you get to choose whether you go to the park or to some special shops. These **choices** might be considered neutral, that is, not necessarily bad or good. You also make **choices** about how you treat people or act around people. You might choose to be kind, which is making a good choice. Or you might choose instead to be mean, which is making a poor choice. There are children who make good **choices**, and there are grownups who make poor **choices**. It doesn't matter how old you are, God can give you the wisdom to do what is right.

God's Scripture time

Get your God's Scripture Time flashcards ready! We are talking about making good **choices** in this lesson, and this verse helps us know that it is good to praise God for making us with such wonder. Choosing to honor and love Him is always a good choice. Now listen to this one last time, then say it with me:

I will praise You, for I am fearfully and wonderfully made; marvelous are Your works, and that my soul knows very well (Psalm 139:14).

Language 07:00 time!

Some people in the world speak a language called Ukrainian. If you want to say "thank you" in Ukranian, you just say *dyakuju* (jah coo joo). Let's say it now, in a light way: *dyakuju*. There are people in a country called Ukraine who speak this language. Why don't you get your continent map of Europe and color in Ukraine!

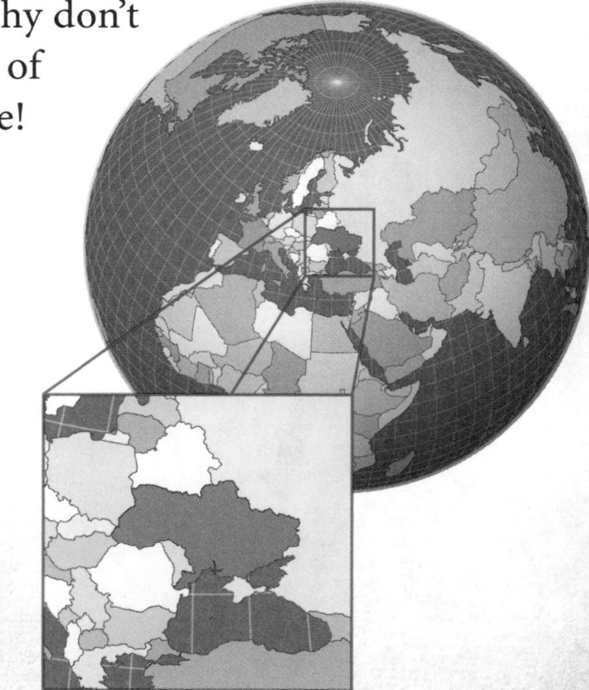

Name

Picture time!

When summer comes, there are some special holidays and festivals that people celebrate around the world. Egemenlik Bayrami is celebrated in April in the country of Turkey, and it celebrates how important children are. Kodomo no hi is celebrated in Japan, with families flying carp-shaped kites from their homes. In India, the festival of Raksha Bandhan is celebrated in August, and in the festival, a sister places a bracelet called a *rakhis* on her brother's wrist to show her love and caring for him.

Color the flying carp-shaped kite below.

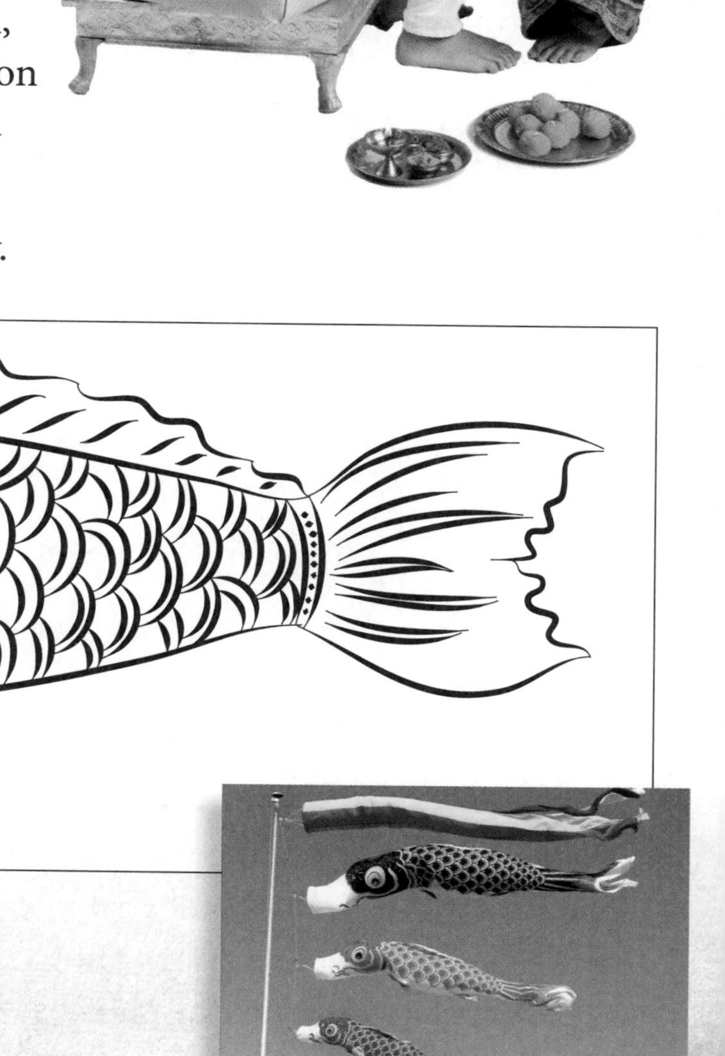

In every community, there are wonderful helpers who make things better for us by making sure we make wise **choices**. These helpers include financial assistants who guide us so we can have the money we need to buy things we want and money enough to retire when we get older. Many older people stop working when they can live off of the money they have saved up, and this is called retirement. Also, there are coaches who help us make healthy choices with the foods we eat and in proper exercising. It's so important to make wise decisions!

Every day you make so many **choices**, from what shirt to wear, to what to eat, to whether you will be kind or not as kind. What are some of the **choices** you've made just today?

Turn to the Lesson 31 My Book Time page in the back of this book to complete your story for the week in words and colors!

In a Sailboat at Sea with All I Need

God Provides for Us

LESSON #32

TEACHER NOTES

Developmental Mile Markers

A Joyful Childhood: The following are some ways to help young children develop habits that teach them how to live a life of joy in God's goodness to us: 1. Give thanks to God at meal times. 2. Prepare meals together. 3. Ask how his or her day was and then listen. 4. Tell stories about your childhood and family history. 5. Teach them how to write personal notes to people. 6. Make sure your child knows you are proud of him or her. 7. Make sure your child has time to just play.

SUPPLIES

- ☐ Crayons or colored pens or pencils

Lesson Goals

Students should be able to:

- Recognize that God provides for us and cares for us deeply.

word collector **Provides**: Gives something to another, such as God providing all we need.

Name

The more we know God, the more we know God is good. Come on, it's go time!

God **provides**. Those two words say so much! He **provides** a way for us to be saved from our sins through Jesus His Son. He **provides** healing for us when we're sick. He **provides** strength for us to work and wisdom for us to make wise choices, and He gives us peace when bad things happen around us. He cares so deeply for us in every way. To know that God **provides** for us is something that can give you joy all your life.

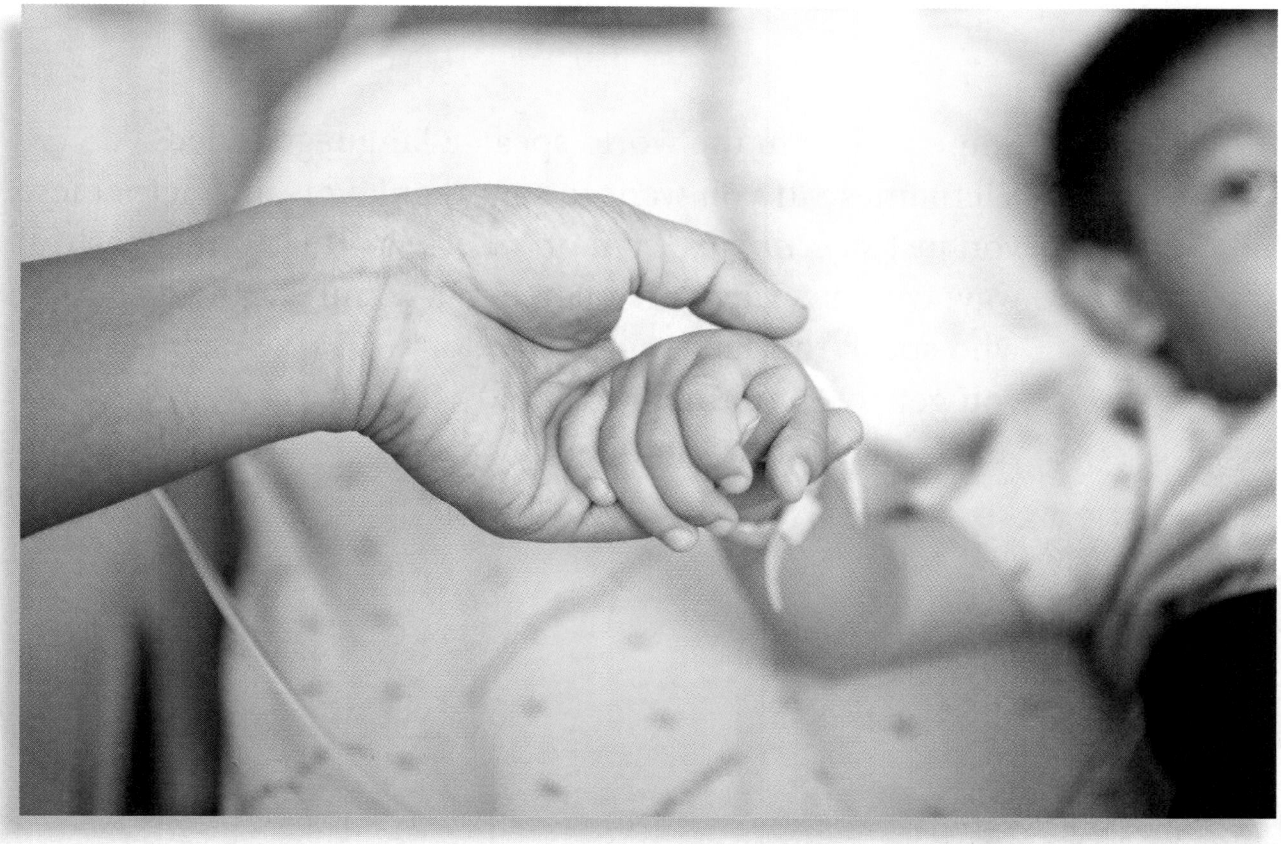

Get your God's Scripture Time flashcards ready! We are talking about how God **provides** for us in this lesson, and this verse helps us keep our focus on praising God for His goodness, for all He **provides** for us. We have endless reasons to rejoice in Him every single day. Now listen to this one last time, then say it with me:

Rejoice in the Lord always. Again I will say, rejoice! (Philippians 4:4).

Language 07:00 time!

Some people in the world speak a language called Vietnamese. If you want to say "thank you" in Vietnamese, you just say *cam on* (cam on). Let's say it now, in a bashful way: *cam on*. There are people in a country called Vietnam who speak this language. Why don't you get your continent map of Asia and color in Vietnam!

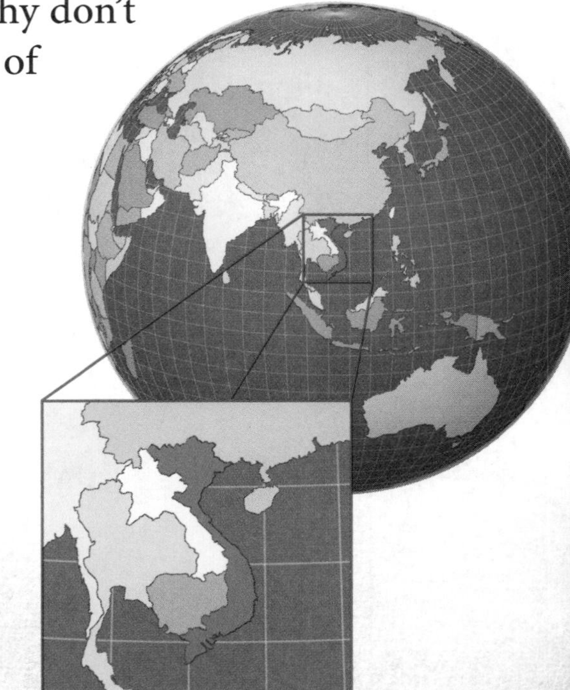

Name

Picture time!

Color in the picture with these things God has given to us.

God is so good. His world is not only beautiful, but through it He gives us all we need to be healthy, to be cared for, and to be full of joy. In every community, there are people who highlight the wonders of God and His nature through what they do. These helpers include photographers who capture glimpses, with a camera, of God's world and those who love Him; painters who give us paintings of God's natural wonders that can be appreciated year after year; and workers at homeless shelters who make sure that all in need find hope and help when they are struggling in the world.

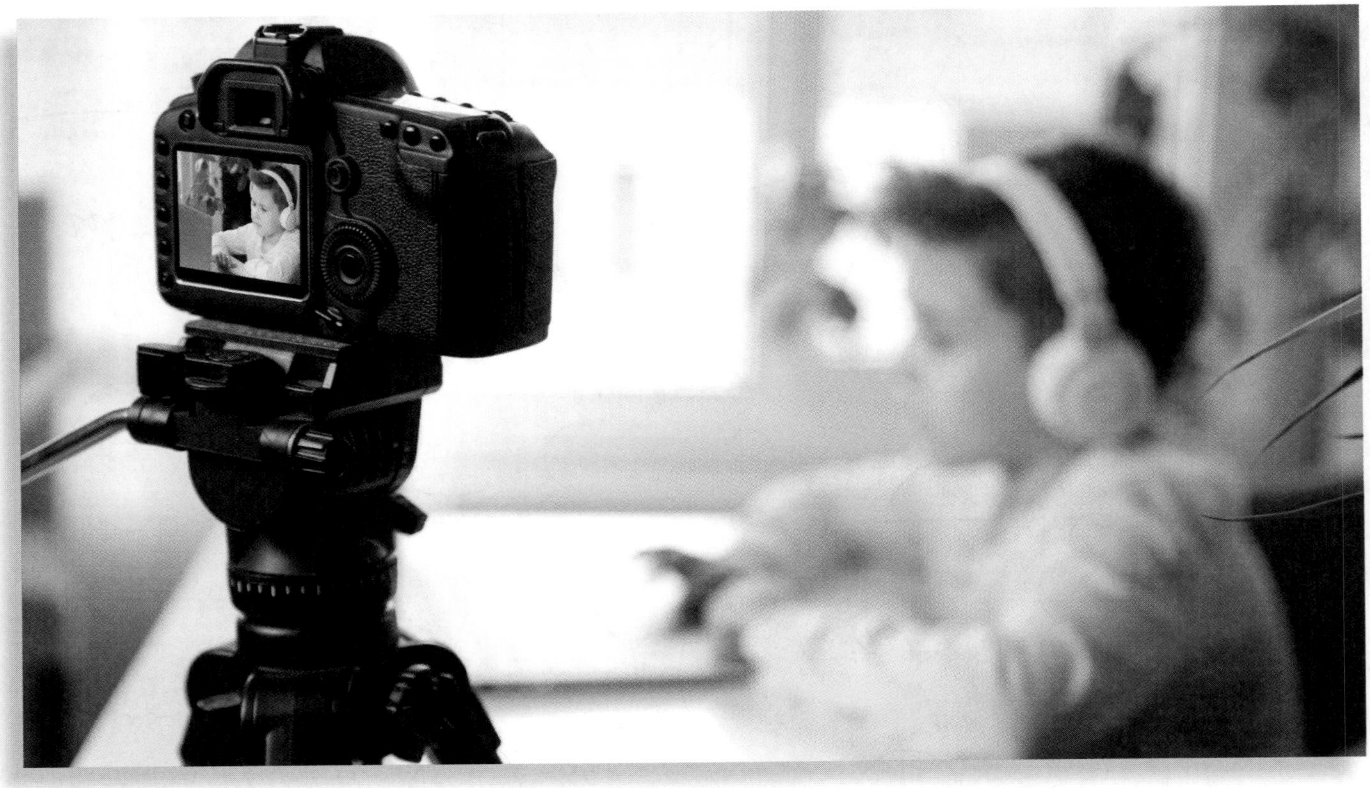

Jesus told us that we shouldn't worry about what we need to eat or drink, or what we need to wear, because God cares so much about us and always **provides** for us. Have you ever worried about things you need? What can you do to have God's peace when you start to get concerned about something?

Turn to the Lesson 32 My Book Time page in the back of this book to complete your story for the week in words and colors!

Over Water or Land an Amphibious Vehicle Will Stand

Environments and Our Needs

LESSON #33

TEACHER NOTES

Developmental Mile Markers

Healthy Sleep: You can help children at night by reading to them before bed, encouraging a love of books, and praying over them before they sleep. A vital need for children, for people at any age, is a restful night's sleep. This helps us regain our strength for each new day, no matter where God has placed us on His earth.

SUPPLIES

- ☐ Crayons or colored pens or pencils

Lesson Goals

Students should be able to:

- Describe how we can all help take care of God's wondrous world.

word collector **Recycle**: To reuse so something is not wasted or thrown away.

Name

Go time!

God provides everything we need! Let's always remember to thank Him. And now, it's go time!

Sometimes we throw things away when we no longer need them. But some things can be recycled or made to be used again. These are some cans, paper, plastic, and cardboard. Are you able to **recycle** things where you live?

Being able to **recycle** is just one thing we can do to help protect the world God created. He provides so much for us and for the animals and plants He created as well. The environment is the area that is around us where we live. The earth was created with all we need to survive, including air to breathe, water to drink, and wood and stone and more we can build houses with. God takes care of us, and we take care of His world.

God's Scripture time

Get your God's Scripture Time flashcards ready! We are talking about environments and our needs in this lesson, and this verse helps us realize that as God provides for us, we can help others and show love to them. Now listen to this one last time, then say it with me:

You shall love your neighbor as yourself (Matthew 22:39).

Language time!

07:00

Some people in the world speak a language called Welsh. If you want to say "thank you" in Welsh, you just say *diolch* (dee olch). Let's say it now, in a quick way: *diolch*. There are people in a country called Wales who speak this language. Why don't you get your continent map of Europe and color in Wales!

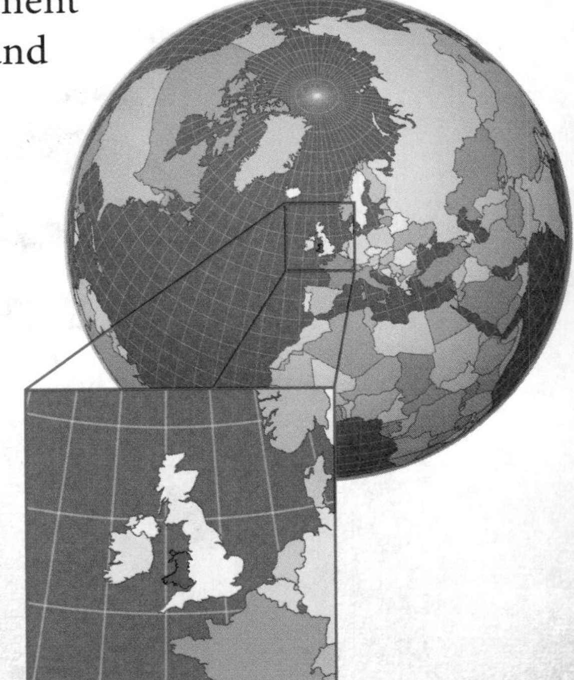

Name

Picture time!

Color this image about recycling below and discuss ways you can help recycle more.

As we are learning, the environment is the world around us, whether we live in the mountains, in a desert, or on the cold tundra. In communities across the world, there are people who help us live happy and healthy lives in any kind of environment. There are heating and air specialists who make sure we can keep our homes and offices at just the right temperature no matter how hot or cold it is outside. There are also people called urban planners who help cities take care of their land, and environmental engineers who try to protect land from harmful chemicals or processes.

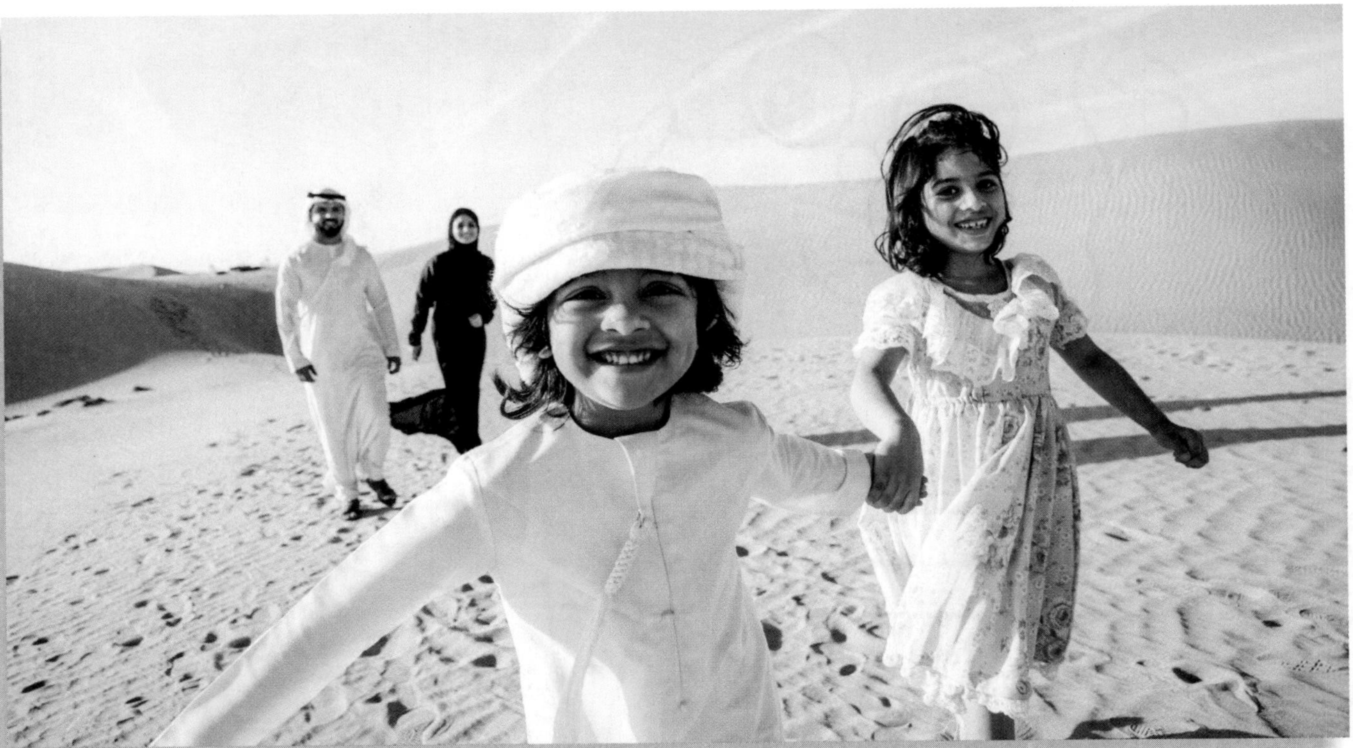

Keeping warm when it's cold, cool when it's hot, or dry when it's raining are things that are possible in our world because of indoor climate controls. Do you prefer being inside in the summer when it's hot outside or inside in the winter when it's cold outside? Why?

Turn to the Lesson 33 My Book Time page in the back of this book to complete your story for the week in words and colors!

A Chinese Junk with a Phone and a Bunk

Goods and Services

LESSON #34

TEACHER NOTES

Developmental Mile Markers

Emotional Health: Help children define their emotions (I am sad) and why they feel a certain way (my friend said something mean to me). Understanding our emotional needs and responses to situations helps us make wise choices that go beyond our temporary emotional states.

SUPPLIES

- ☐ Crayons or colored pens or pencils

Lesson Goals

Students should be able to:

- Compare and contrast the differences between goods and services

word collector **Services**: Things people do for you that you pay them for (like a haircut).

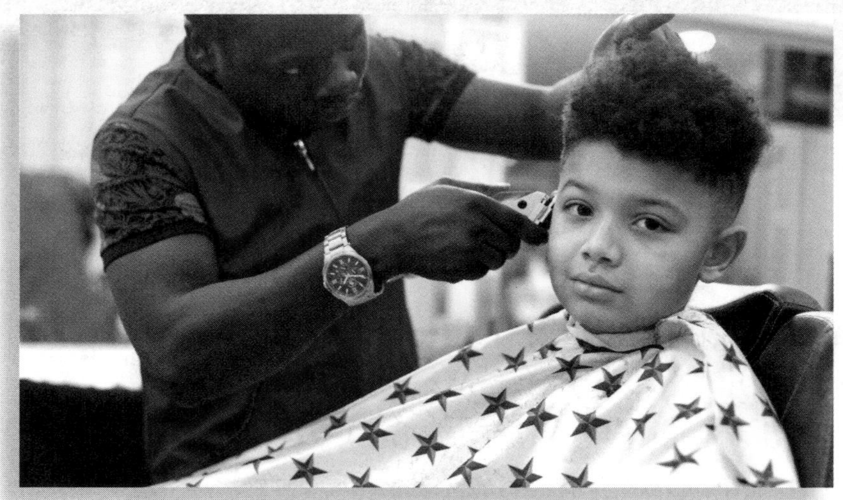

Name ______________________________

It's another week in God's wondrous world. It's go time!

We have talked about buying, borrowing, or trading things. Well, goods are products you can buy (like books), while **services** are not things you can touch, but things people do for you (like haircuts). We usually pay for goods and **services**, but let's see if you can tell them apart. Look at the pictures. Now, circle whether the place shown provides some good or product or if it provides some service instead.

How did you do?

BARBERSHOP Goods Service	 TOYS Goods Service
 Market Goods Service	 BANK Goods Service

Get your God's Scripture Time flashcards ready! We are talking about goods and **services** in this lesson, and this verse helps us realize that loving God and loving others is not a hard thing. He provides ways for us to have what we need, sometimes through various goods or **services**, and we can help others too by loving them. Now listen to this one last time, then say it with me:

For this is the love of God, that we keep His commandments. And His commandments are not burdensome (1 John 5:3).

Language time!

07:00

Some people in the world speak a language called Xhosa. If you want to say "thank you" in Xhosa, you just say *enkosi* (in co see). Let's say it now, in a loud way: *enkosi*. There are people in a country called South Africa who speak this language. Why don't you get your continent map of Africa and color in South Africa!

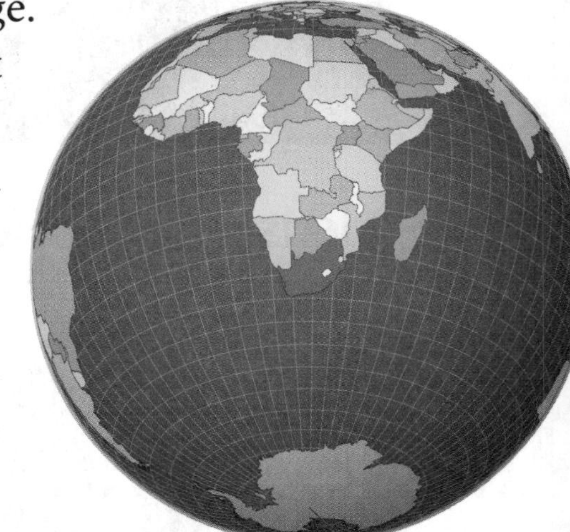

Name

Picture time!

Draw a line from the vehicle to the way it delivers goods.

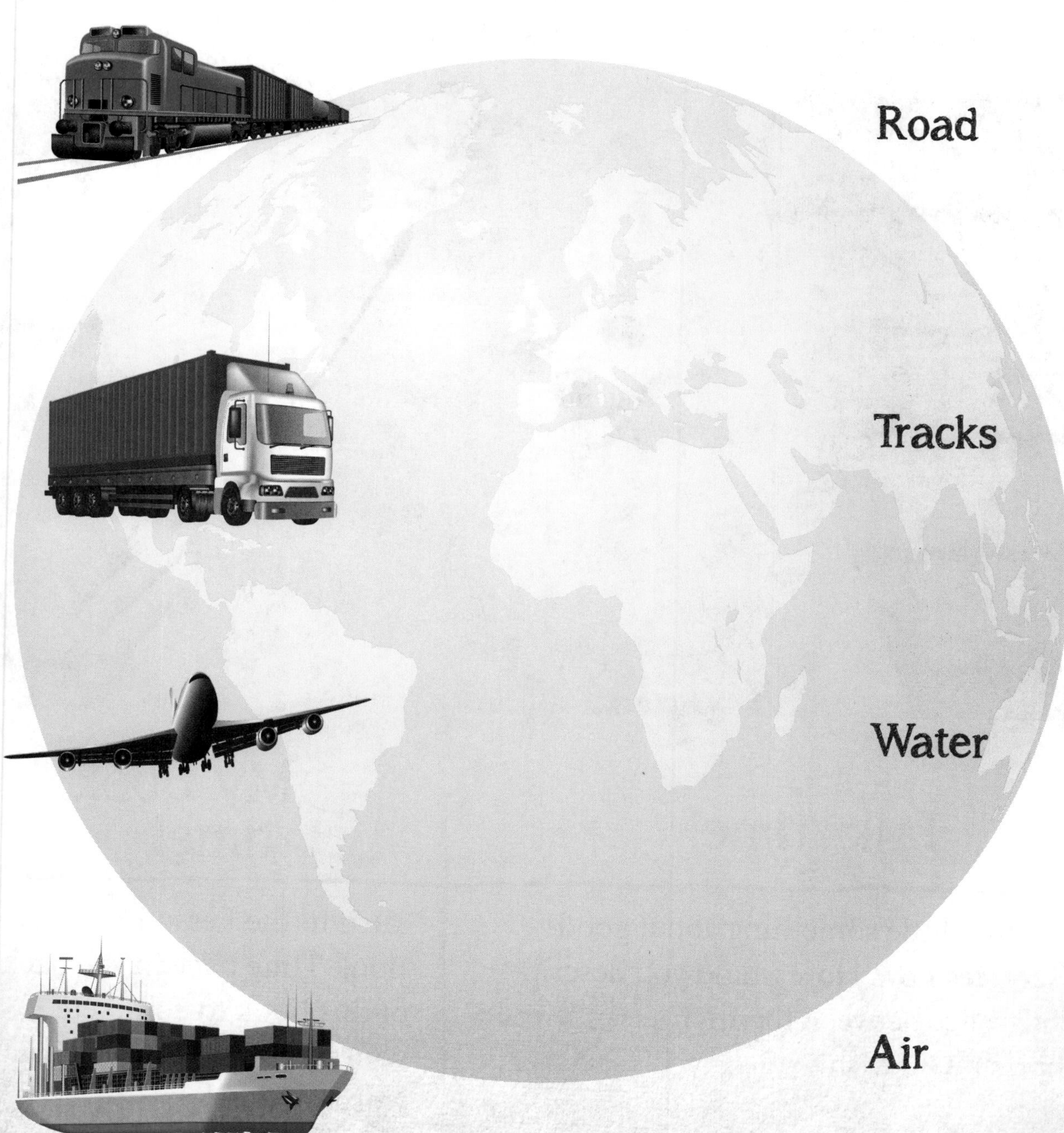

As we talk about goods and **services**, let's look at our local towns and cities to see the helpers there who provide wonderful things for us! If you have a dog that sometimes sheds or simply has hair that gets long and wild, you might need the service of a pet groomer. If you have a business and need some extra help to know how to run it, you might need the service of a consultant. If you want someone to feel really special, you might send him or her some flowers, and a florist provides this for us. Or if you want to buy some special teas, a tea shop might have just the goods you're looking for!

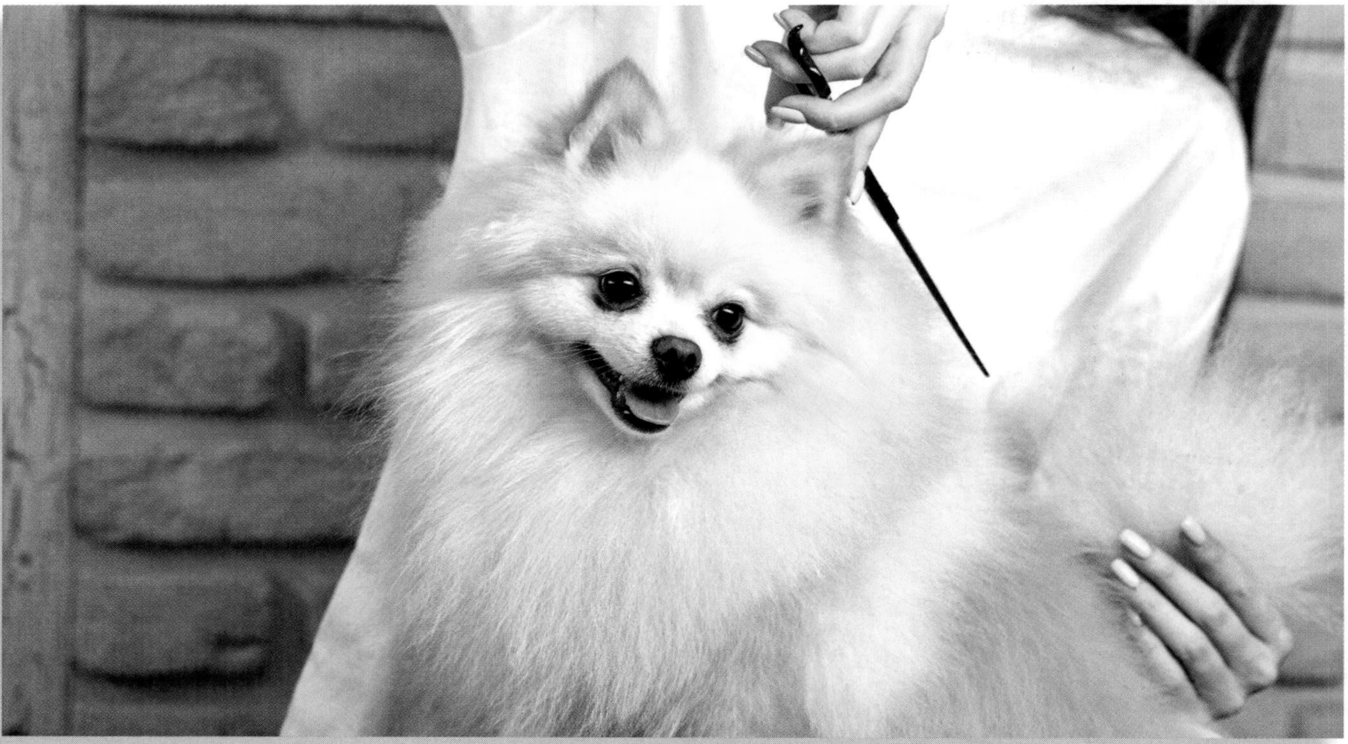

You know a little something about goods and **services** now. How would you describe the difference between them? You can use examples if you wish!

Turn to the Lesson 34 My Book Time page in the back of this book to complete your story for the week in words and colors!

On a Dinghy to Work for Those Around Me

Chores and Jobs

LESSON #35

TEACHER NOTES

Developmental Mile Markers

Learning: It's so important to teach children a love of learning. Let learning be fun, something that you are enthusiastic about. Teach with a variety of activities so they are challenged in various ways. This can also be an important lesson with chores, finding joy in a job well done, or even just picking up toys before bed.

SUPPLIES

- ☐ Crayons or colored pens or pencils

Lesson Goals

Students should be able to:

- Identify the importance of helping around the house and how this can lead to good habits for when you get a job.

word collector **Work**: Something you do to help others or to earn money.

Name ______________________________

Let's get ready for the new week. It's go time!

Families do so much to keep everyone cared for. Sometimes the load can feel so heavy. So anytime you can pitch in to help, that would be something much appreciated. Just keeping your things picked up or helping with chores is a good thing.

The more you learn to **work** with a good attitude around the house, the more you will learn to one day perhaps work outside your house when you're older. What you learn when you are young helps carry over into what you need later on. You will learn to **work** hard for you, for others, and for God.

Color the picture of the girl doing her chores.

Get your God's Scripture Time flashcards ready! We are talking about chores and jobs in this lesson, and this verse helps us realize that in all you do now and in all you will do one day, you can trust in the Lord completely, and He will give you the wisdom and knowledge you need. Now listen to this one last time, then say it with me:

Trust in the Lord with all your heart, and lean not on your own understanding . . . (Proverbs 3:5).

Language 07:00 time!

Some people in the world speak a language called Yoruba. If you want to say "thank you" in Yoruba, you just say *e se* (ee see). Let's say it now, in a big way: *e se*. There are people in a country called Nigeria who speak this language. Why don't you get your continent map of Africa and color in Nigeria!

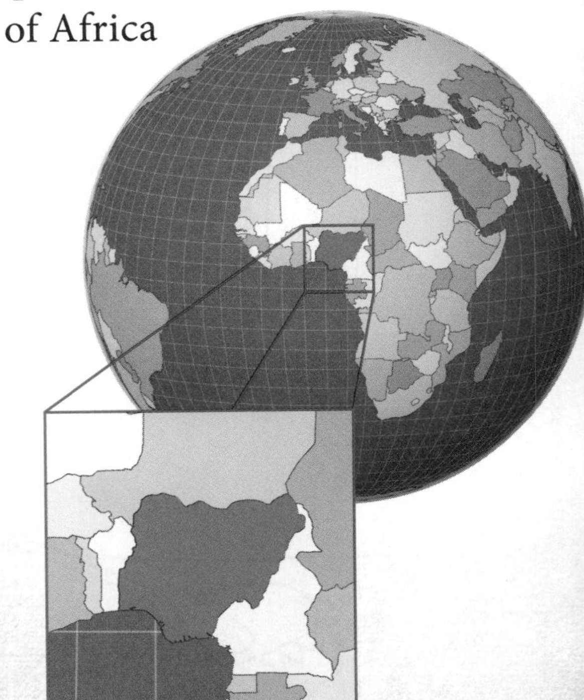

Name

Picture time!

Color in the items below that are used to assist us with our chores and talk about all you do to help your family around the house.

When we're young, there aren't always as many things we can do to earn money. Sometimes you can earn some by doing chores around the house. When we get a little older, there are more ways we can be helpers for people in our neighborhood. You might be able to mow lawns of neighbors on your street in the summer, help rake up their leaves in the autumn, shovel the snow on their sidewalks in the winter, or help them with their yard **work** in the spring. We can all be good neighbor helpers!

What you learn while doing chores around the house can help you at your job when you are all grown up. When you're asked to do things to help out around the house, do you do it with a good heart? This is something you can choose to do all your life.

Turn to the Lesson 35 My Book Time page in the back of this book to complete your story for the week in words and colors!

Surfing Away to a Place I Want to Stay

Different Careers

TEACHER NOTES

End of week recipe ingredients:

- ☐ 2 ripe mangoes
- ☐ 1 lime
- ☐ 1 teaspoon of honey
- ☐ 2/3 cup whipping cream
- ☐ 5 oz plain yogurt
- ☐ 1 tablespoon coconut milk

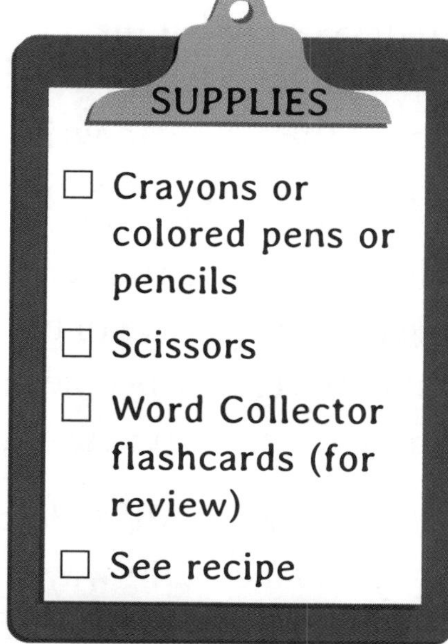

Developmental Mile Markers Review

Choices: As children grow older, give them more choices to help them mature in making decisions. This might include choosing what to wear, what games to play, or what to have as a snack. It will eventually help them learn to distinguish between the value of needs and wants.

Solving Problems: If your child becomes upset about a situation, make sure to help him or her work through simple problem-solving steps if there is anything he or she might do to help make things better. Just as we learn to choose between what is most needed and what is simply a want, we also learn that our responses to situations are also ours to choose.

Self-worth: Parents and teachers can help young children develop their esteem by giving praise for things they accomplish, encouraging them to do new things, establishing realistic goals, and by not being overly critical to them. One way this can be fostered is through simple, age-appropriate work around the house, possibly getting an allowance for work done well, and then guiding the children to save or spend responsibly.

Healthy Emotions: You can help children develop healthy emotional responses by understanding that they may act out until they learn to control their emotions, listening to their worries and fears, and letting them speak about their emotions without putting them down. Ultimately, we all choose our response to situations, and God can give us the grace and peace to choose wisely.

A Joyful Childhood: The following are some ways to help young children develop habits that teach them how to live a life of joy in God's goodness to us: 1. Give thanks to God at meal times. 2. Prepare meals together. 3. Ask how his or her day was and then listen. 4. Tell stories about your childhood and family history. 5. Teach them how to write personal notes to people. 6. Make sure your child knows you are proud of him or her. 7. Make sure your child has time to just play.

Healthy Sleep: You can help children at night by reading to them before bed, encouraging a love of books, and praying over them before they sleep. A vital need for children, for people at any age, is a restful night's sleep. This helps us regain our strength for each new day, no matter where God has placed us on His earth.

Emotional Health: Help children define their emotions (I am sad) and why they feel a certain way (my friend said something mean to me). Understanding our emotional needs and responses to situations helps us make wise choices that go beyond our temporary emotional states.

Learning: It's so important to teach children a love of learning. Let learning be fun, something that you are enthusiastic about. Teach with a variety of activities so they are challenged in various ways. This can also be an important lesson with chores, finding joy in a job well done, or even just picking up toys before bed.

Lesson Goals

Students should be able to:

- Describe various kinds of jobs and how we can find a job that will give us joy as we honor the Lord in all we do.

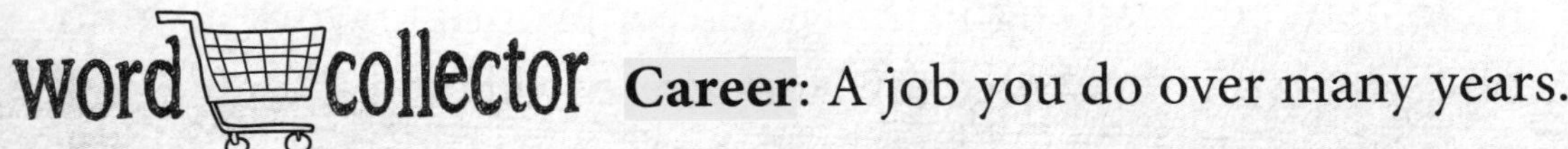

Career: A job you do over many years.

Name

Go time!

We've come to the end of the last quest. Just one more week for go time!

It will be a long time before you would ever have to decide what you might like to do as an adult. So this week, just try and imagine what might have made other people decide what kind of helper they would like to be in their community. Some work in their homes to care for their families, some volunteer outside their homes, some take jobs to earn money or get experience. These are decisions God will give you peace about and wisdom to choose when the time comes.

Color the pictures of the various people in their careers. Can you name them all?

God's Scripture time

Get your God's Scripture Time flashcards ready! We are talking about having a **career** in this lesson, and this verse helps us realize that no matter what you end up doing in your life, you should believe in Jesus and should love others. Now listen to this one last time, then say it with me:

And this is His commandment: that we should believe on the name of His Son Jesus Christ and love one another, as He gave us commandment (1 John 3:23).

Language 07:00 time!

Some people in the world speak a language called Zulu. If you want to say "thank you" in Zulu, you just say *ngiyabona* (gee aw bone ah). Let's say it now, in a quiet way: *ngiyabona.* There are people in a country called Swaziland who speak this language. Why don't you get your continent map of Africa and color in Swaziland!

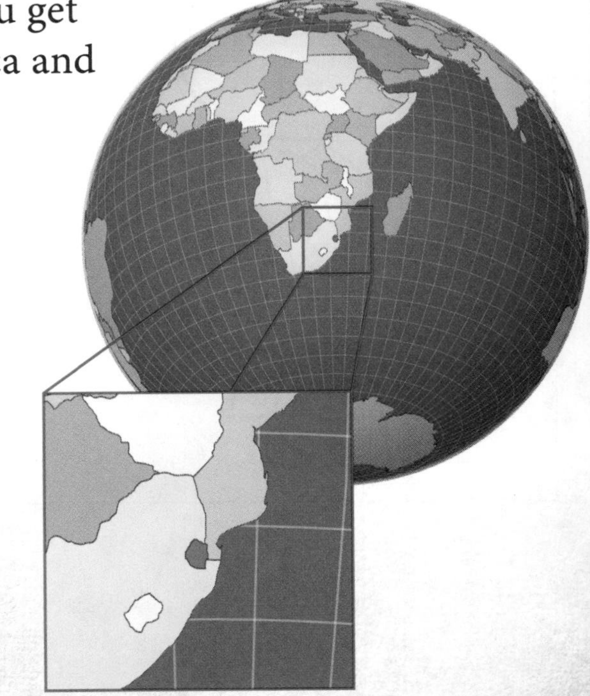

Name

Picture time!

Draw a line from the picture of the child to the profession he or she represents.

Plumber

Builder

Cook

Beautician

Helping hands time!

We can all be helpers, no matter how young we are, and all grow up to be helping hands for those around us. Here in this very last week, let's look at just a few more helpers who make our world a little better! If you need help with your business or your taxes, you might just need the help of an accountant. If you need help with your wedding day, you might just want the help of a wedding planner. And finally, if you want to be lifted by some good live music, you might look for a musical artist near you. There are so many wonderful helpers that God puts in our communities!

Talk time!

What are some possible careers you might like to do when you grow up? Why do these particular jobs seem like a good thing to you?

My Book time!

Turn to the Lesson 36 My Book Time page in the back of this book to complete your story for the week in words and colors!

Food Time

Fruit Around the World!

Fruit, like the other staples we've discussed, comes from all over the world. Fruits develop from the flower of the plant and have seeds. They can grow on trees, vines, shrubs, or bushes. Types of fruit that grow on trees are apples, oranges, mangoes, lemons, coconuts, bananas, and pears. Fruit can also grow on vines. Grapes, raspberries, blackberries, melons, and kiwis come from vines. Strawberries, gooseberries, and blueberries are found on shrubs. Fruits contain many nutrients and vitamins we need to live and grow and are best eaten raw or uncooked. Fruits also make delicious desserts such as pies, cookies, and cakes.

What types of fruit are your favorites? Look around in your kitchen. Where do you keep your fruit? What kinds do you have in your house? Is there a fruit listed that you want to try this week?

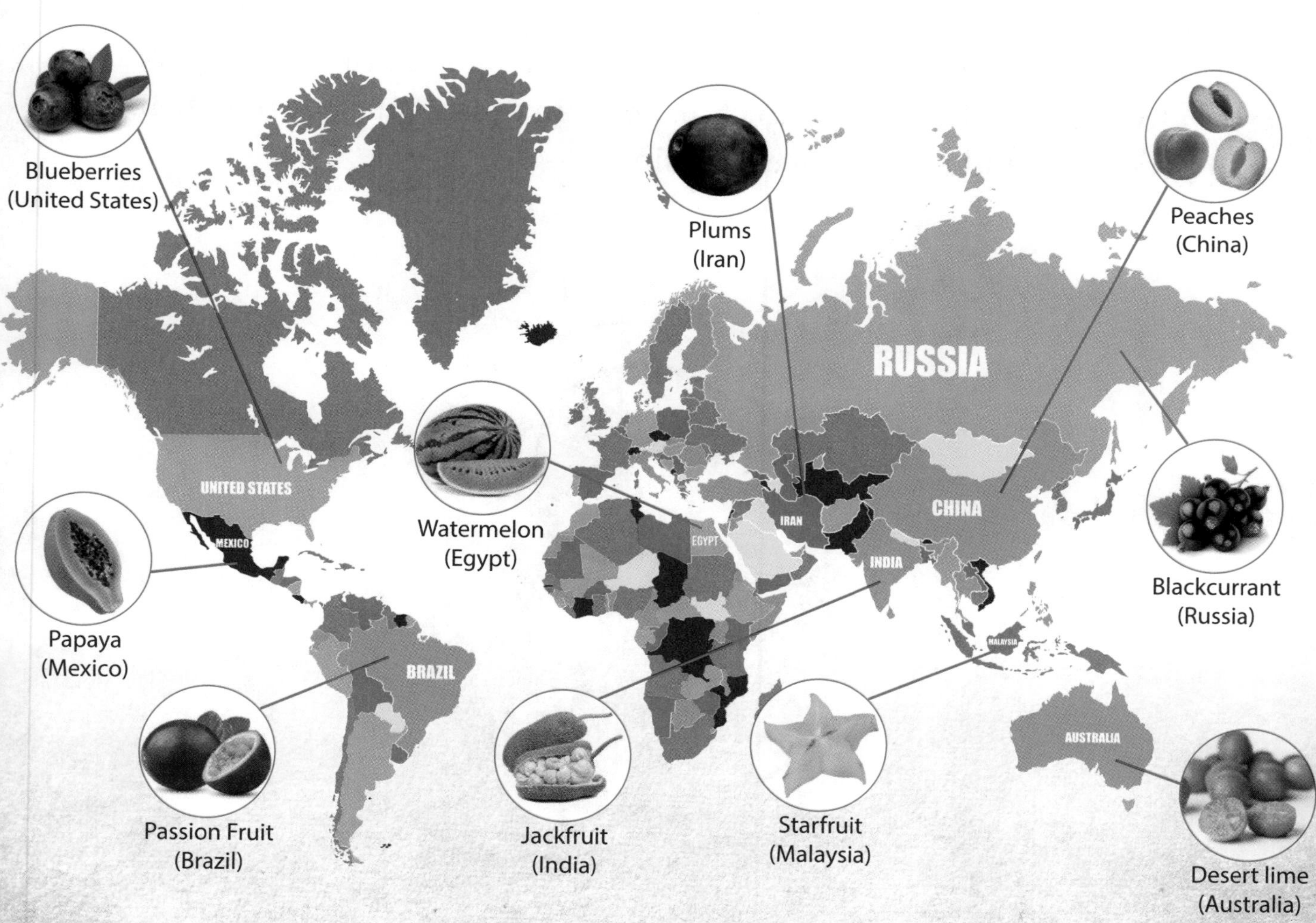

Here's a recipe to try and make with your teacher:

Mango Fool

Caribbean and Africa

Ingredients

- ☐ 2 ripe mangoes
- ☐ 1 lime
- ☐ 1 teaspoon of honey
- ☐ 2/3 cup whipping cream
- ☐ 5 oz plain yogurt
- ☐ 1 tablespoon coconut milk

Slice mango into small cubes. Place the mango in a bowl and mash with a fork until it is smooth. Cut and juice the lime. Combine the fresh lime juice and honey into the mashed mango and mix well.

In a separate bowl, whisk the whipping cream until it just starts to thicken. Pour in the yogurt and coconut milk into the mango mixture. Gently fold the cream to combine. Refrigerate to chill. Serve in dessert cups or bowls. Top with whipped cream and mango slice, if desired.

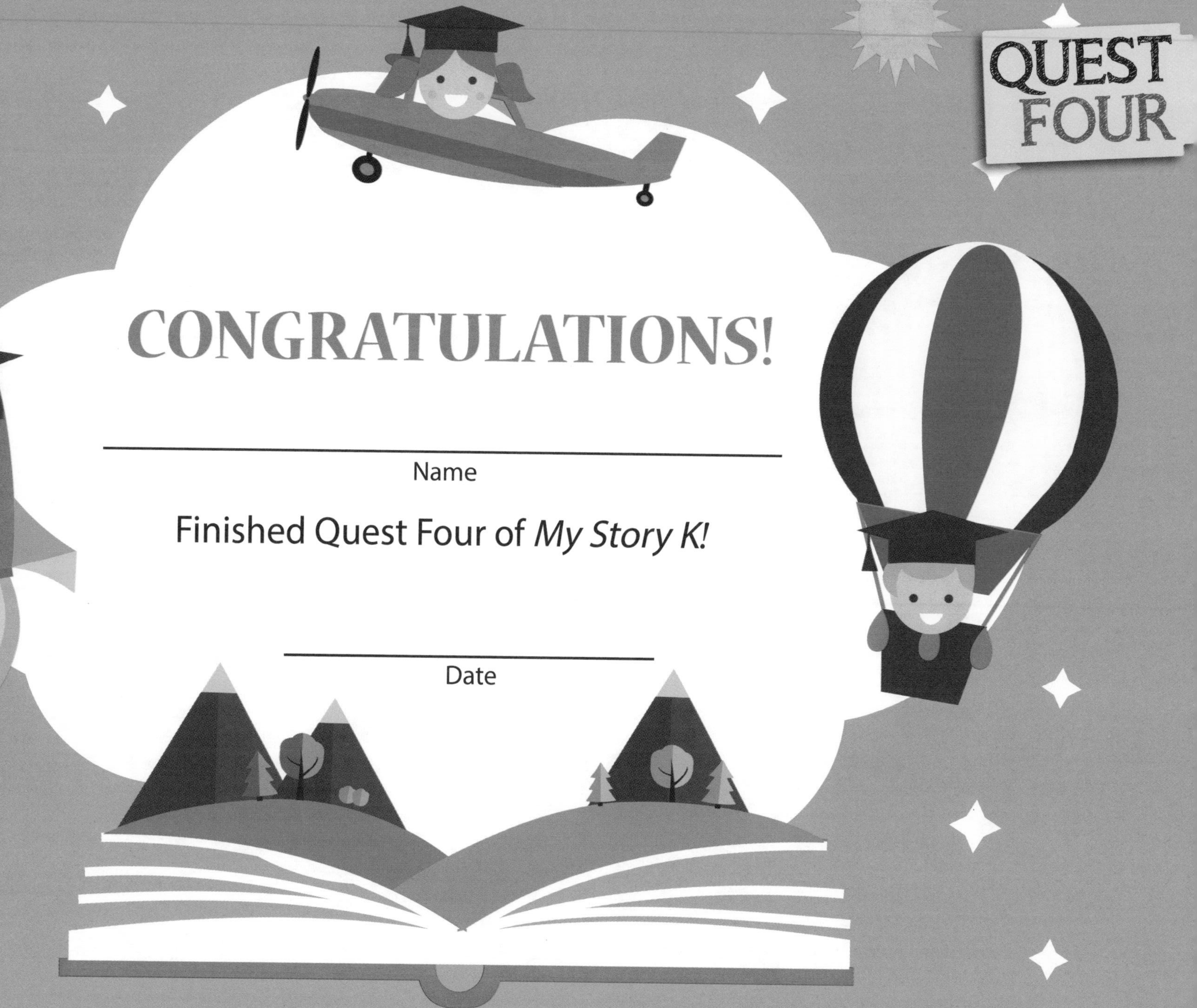
QUEST FOUR
CONGRATULATIONS!
Name
Finished Quest Four of *My Story K!*
Date

My Book time!

by

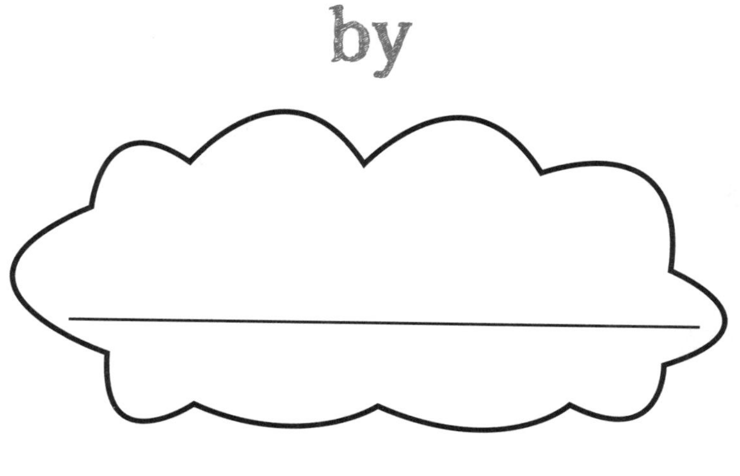

My Family and Me

1. Student's first name Annabelle
2. Day of birthday (e.g., 3rd) 1 - 27 - 2017
3. Month of birthday January

1. Annabelle stood there next to a wall,
And seemed so incredibly tall.
For a birthday was near,
Everyone soon would cheer,
On the 2. 27 of
3. January, they'd have a ball!

Color the birthday cake and draw in the candles to show how old you are.

Where We Live

LESSON #2

1. Student's first name ______________________________

2. Student is a boy or girl (write "his" OR "her") ____________

3. Name of street student lives on ________________________________

4. Hometown ____

1. ____________________________ knew the way to 2. ________ home,

And knew never to walk all alone.

3. ________________________________ was the street,

Kind neighbors there to greet,

In 4. ____,

where joyfulness was known.

Color the picture of the boy helping a lady cross the street.

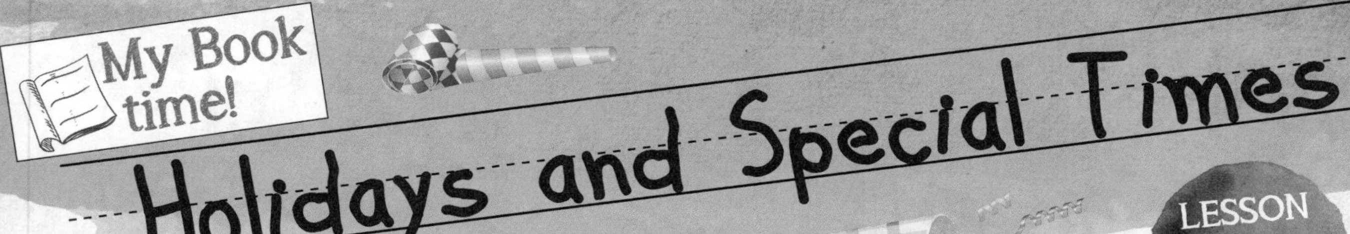

Holidays and Special Times

1. Student's first name______________________________
2. A favorite holiday________________________________
3. A favorite thing about the holiday____________________________

1. ______________________________ loved 2. ______________________________
the best,
and celebrating with family was so blessed.
The 3. ______________________________ was/were so wondrous,
all the day brought such peace thus,
what a time for so much joy to be expressed!

Draw a picture of your favorite thing from your favorite holiday.

Good Food and Nutrition

1. Name of market or shop you buy food from ____________________
2. Student's first name ____________________________
3. A favorite meal ________________________________

At 1. _______________________ 2. ____________________ went to go shop

For 3. ________________________ and some veggies to chop.

There was lots of good stuff,

Healthy fruits, breads, and a cream puff,

Wondrous things are now coming nonstop!

Color the picture of the different fruits.

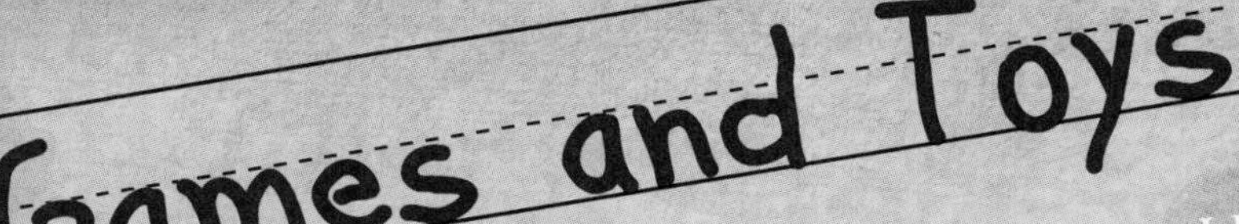

LESSON #5

1. A friend's name ______________________________
2. A favorite game ______________________________
3. Student's first name ______________________________

1. ______________________________ was coming over about ten
to play 2. ______________________________ with
3. ______________________________ in the den.
The game lasted an hour,
they ate snacks that were both sweet and sour,
then they did it all over again!

Draw a picture of your favorite game.

Clothing and Uniforms

1. Student's first name ______________________________

2. Helping hands person who wears a uniform _____________________

3. A warm pie you like _________________________

1. ______________________________ went to a park in the fall

To see a parade and play some baseball.

A 2. _____________________ walked by,

eating a plate of warm 3. _________________________ pie,

Going to stand by the large painted wall.

Color this picture of a pie and choose the correct colors to make it your favorite kind of pie.

Music and Song

LESSON #7

1. Student's first name ______________________________
2. A family member's name ______________________________
3. A friend's name ______________________________

1. ______________________________ started to sing a loud song,
While 2. ______________________________ and
3. ______________________________ both sang along.
First, the neighbors could hear,
then the town's puppeteer,
Until all of it ended quite strong!

Color the picture of the puppeteer's puppet.

Pictures and Words in Books

LESSON #8

1. Student's first name ______________________________
2. A favorite book ____
3. The current month ______________________________

While 1. ______________________________ read
2. ____ in the park,
the sky started turning quite dark.
It was 3. ______________________________ of that year,
soon the moon would appear
behind clouds that looked like a shark!

Have your teacher take a photograph of you holding your favorite book and place it below.

Glue or tape photograph here.

Reading and Writing

1. Student's first name ______________________
2. A favorite color ________________
3. A favorite place you visit ________________________

While writing a new book with a pen,

1. ____________________ saw a small 2. ______________ wren.

The bird flew into the sky

and soon soared back by,

for 3. ______________________ it would call home again.

Color the picture of the wren below.

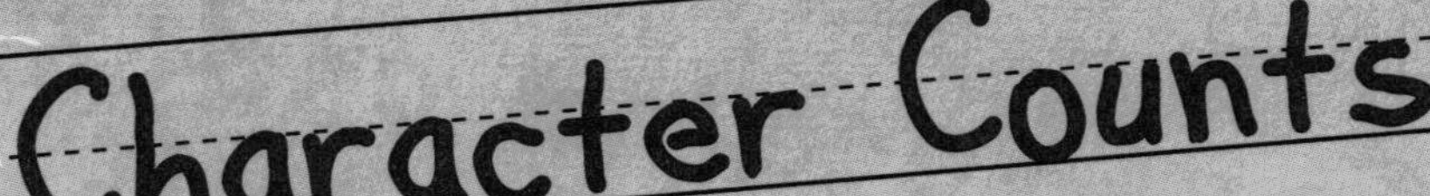

1. Student's first name ______________________________

2. A good character trait (like helpful, giving, etc.)

____

1. ______________________________ always tried to be
2. ______________________________ and kind,
for these were things no one would mind.
To give help in a pinch
was always a cinch
for a heart so polished and shined!

Tell your teacher five ways that you can show kindness to others.

1. ____
2. ____
3. ____
4. ____
5. ____

Keeping Us Safe

1. Student's first name ______________________________
2. Something about a fire that can hurt us ________________________

Now 1. ______________________________ heard the fire alarm

And knew the 2. ________________________ could cause so much harm.

So without hesitation,

1. ______________________________ sprang into action

and woke everyone on the farm.

Saving everyone on the farm makes you a superhero. Color the superhero here.

God Protects Us

1. Student's first name ______________________________
2. Something you're afraid of ______________________________

God keeps 1. ______________________________ safe in His love,

that comes down from heaven above.

If 2. ______________________________ come(s) to threaten,

God's love will get right in;

we can know that it fits like a glove.

Tell your teacher five ways that God keeps you safe.

1. ____
2. ____
3. ____
4. ____
5. ____

Traditions Around the World

1. Student's first name ______________________________

2. Joyful tradition/holiday your family celebrates ______________________________

3. Celebrate mostly in the day OR night ______________________________

1. ______________________________ thought
2. ______________________________ was quite keen
and so much better than the simple routine.
Whatever the weather,
the 3. ______________________________ only got better;
one just smiled like a king or a queen!

Draw a picture of a tradition at your house.

My Friends and Me

LESSON #14

1. Student's first name ______________________________

2. A good friend ______________________________

3. Another good friend ______________________________

4. Something you enjoy eating with your friends

____

1. ______________________________ went outside to play
With 2. ______________________________ and
3. ______________________________ all day.
They ate 4. ______________________________ for lunch,
on it all day did they munch,
and by evening, they had so much to say!

Tell your teacher five of your favorite games to play.

1. ____

2. ____

3. ____

4. ____

5. ____

Resolving Conflict

1. Student's first name ______________________________

2. Pick angry OR sad_________________________

1.______________________ was upset quite a bit,

for someone had thrown a big fit.

1.________________ was 2._______________ at night,

But by first morning light,

God helped both of them to just cool it.

Color the picture of the girl waking up in a good mood.

Community Leaders

1. Student's first name ______________________________
2. A leader in your community ______________________________
3. A good leader's trait (gentleness, kindness, etc.)

____

1. ______________________________ would meet
2. ______________________________ today,

for the leader had a nice giveaway.

All who showed 3. ______________________________ and joy

received a shining new toy,

and better yet, the whole group would pray!

Have your teacher take a photograph of you with your favorite toy and place it below.

Glue or tape photograph here.

Heroes and Helpers

1. Student's first name ______________________________
2. A community hero job you might want to do one day

____

1. ______________________________ wished to be a(n)
2. ______________________________ one day,

though a lot of work would be needed, they say.
One must study and grow;
there is so much to know
to be a hero or helper that way!

Color the patrol car and the ambulance below.

Citizens of Heaven

1. Student's first name ______________________________
2. A place that helps people in need get food ____________________

1. ______________________________ goes to help people in need,
to 2. ____________________, precious families to feed.
For God loves us all,
the big and the small,
so we're most like Him as we love, indeed!

Tell your teacher five ways your family can help others in need.

1. ____
2. ____
3. ____
4. ____
5. ____

Local Life

1. Student's first name ______________________
2. A favorite place to go locally ______________________
3. Favorite thing to get there ______________________

1. ______________________ loved life in the fall
And often went to (the) 2. ______________________ by the wall.
For everyone had so much fun,
And the 3. ______________________ was/were second to none.
All those who came had such a ball.

Color the picture of the leaf.
Be sure to give it fall colors.

1. Student's first name ______________________________

2. Student is boy or girl (write he OR she) ____________

3. North OR south ______________________

1. ______________________________ was feeling quite thrilled,

For soon 2. __________ was going to build

a sandcastle at the lake,

then a three-level cake,

in the fridge far 3. _________________ it would be chilled.

Follow the correct street so each car is at the house of the same color.

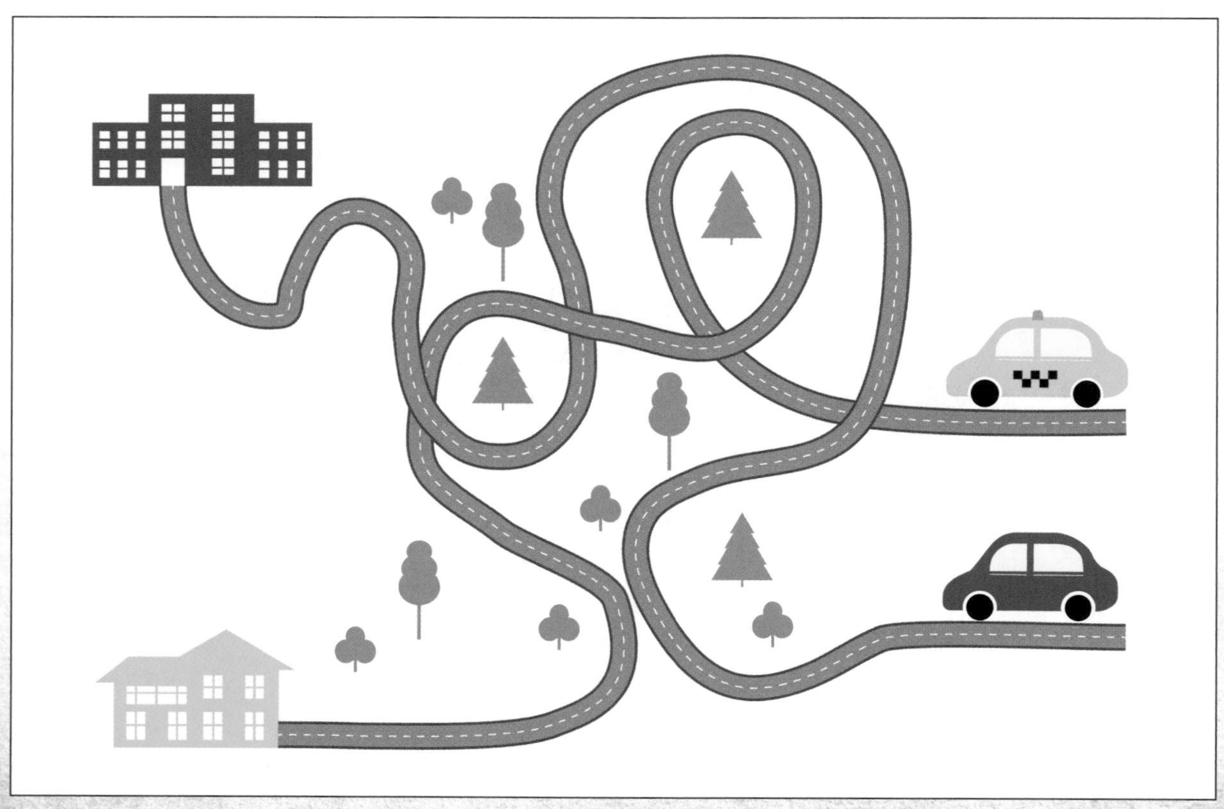

Community

1. Student's first name ______________________________

2. A favorite place to go in your community __________________________

Now 1. _____________________________ loved the wonderful town,

Especially the 2. _________________________ that was brown.

And though it was late,

they were unable to wait,

so the whole family got set and drove down.

Have your teacher take a photograph of you in front of your favorite place in your community and attach it below.

Glue or tape photograph here.

Rural and Urban Worlds

1. Student's first name ______________________________
2. A favorite sport or game ______________________________

1. ______________________________ loved lots of games in the den,

and other fun things that were in.

No matter the season,

there was always a good reason

to play 2. ______________________________, lose or win.

Color the picture of these girls playing soccer.

My Book time!

Different People of the World

LESSON #23

1. Student's first name ______________________________

2. A favorite way to say "thank you" that you have learned

____

3. Name of the language this is from ______________________________

1. ______________________________ often looked up with surprise,

Saying 2. ______________________________ to God for the skies.

This thank you was said,

in 3. ______________________________ it was read,

for in any language we can learn to be wise.

Tell your teacher five things that you are thankful for.

1. ____

2. ____

3. ____

4. ____

5. ____

Different Parts of the World

LESSON #24

1. Student's first name ______________________________

2. Nearest river to your home ______________________________

1. ______________________________ sought to climb places quite high,
and then to some deserts quite dry.
The 2. ______________________________ was fun too,
as was every sweet view;
just look at that blue butterfly!

Draw a picture of a blue butterfly in the box below.

What the World Eats

LESSON #25

1. Student's first name ______________________________

2. A favorite fruit or vegetable ______________________________

3. A favorite dessert ______________________________

1. ______________________________ woke in a very good mood,

Thinking of 2. ______________________________, such a very good food.

Though some people eat dates

or other things on their plates,

soon 3. ______________________________ would come into view.

Color the box of fruits and vegetables below.

Geography Terms

1. Student's first name ______________________________

2. A favorite vacation place ______________________________

1. ______________________________ ran to the forest of trees,

Hoping to hear the waves of the sea.

Though 2. ______________________________ was not far

by airplane or car,

for now, all felt good with the breeze.

Have your teacher or family member take a photograph of you at your favorite vacation place and attach it below.

Glue or tape photograph here.

Weather Words

1. Student's first name ______________________
2. A favorite season ______________________
3. A favorite thing about that season ______________________

1. ______________________ was okay with the warm
and was even all right with a storm.
But said 2. ______________________ was the best,
where all felt quite blessed
because 3. ______________________ was perfect to form.

Tell your teacher five more things you like best about your favorite season.

1. ______________________
2. ______________________
3. ______________________
4. ______________________
5. ______________________

What a Family Needs

1. Student's first name ______________________________
2. Student is a boy or girl (write his OR her) __________
3. A need your family has __________________________

1. _____________________ had hoped for more peace
When 2. __________ family's 3. __________________________ increased.
They prayed for direction
and God's strong protection,
then got them some warm winter fleece.

A family needs heat in the winter. Color the warm fireplace.

Needs Versus Wants

LESSON #29

1. Student's first name ______________________________

2. An essential food or drink ______________________________

1. ______________________________ came over to read

about how 2. ______________________________ was a need.

1. ______________________________ hoped then to ride

A spinning carnival slide;

It was called the Wild Centipede.

Tell your teacher three essential foods and/or drinks.

1. ____

2. ____

3. ____

Trade, Borrow, or Purchase

1. Student's first name ______________________________
2. Something you would like to buy ______________________
3. Student is a boy or girl (his OR her) ___________________

Once 1. ______________________________ went outside to buy
A 2. ______________________ that had caught 3. _____________ eye.
But instead they said just borrow
the 2. ______________________ 'til tomorrow
and really never quite said just why.

Draw a picture of something you would like to buy in the box below.

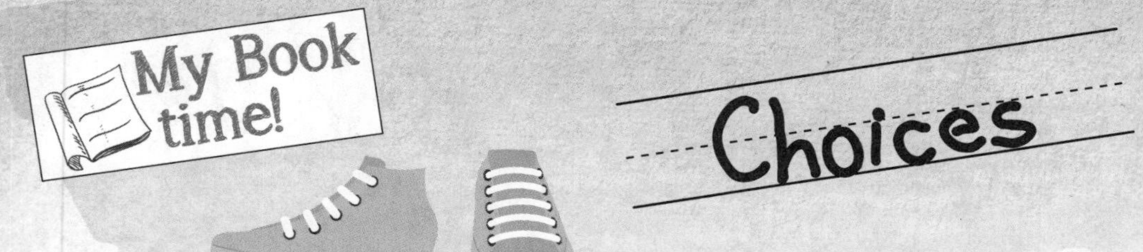

1. Student's first name ______________________

2. A favorite store ______________________

1. ______________________ woke from an afternoon snooze

And was told to prepare to buy shoes.

They headed to the 2. ______________________ store,

found a good pair on the wood floor,

now there was only the laces to choose.

Color the picture of tennis shoes.

God Provides for Us

1. Student's first name ______________________________

2. A favorite thing to do when sick ______________________________

3. Student is a boy or girl (write he OR she) ______________

1. ______________________________ was always quite good,

helping the family throughout childhood.

And once when sick with the flu,

did 2. ______________________________ and pray to come through,

rising as fast as 3. ______________ could.

Draw a picture of your favorite thing to do when you are sick.

Environments and Our Needs

LESSON #33

1. Student's first name ______________________

2. Kind of home you live in ______________________

1. ______________________ didn't mind the hot or the cold

But did love the 2. ______________________, I was told.

Whether summer or fall,

The 2. ______________________ protected them all

And was worth its weight in pure gold.

Have your teacher or parent take a photograph in front of your home and place it below.

Glue or tape photograph here.

Goods and Services

1. Student's first name ______________________________

2. A good or service in your town ___________________________

1. ______________________________ had some things to discuss,

About whether 2. ___________________________ was a good or service.

Was it something you kept

Or something done while you slept?

Sometimes it could make one quite nervous.

Color the plumber. He is the man that services your sink.

Chores and Jobs

1. Student's first name ____________________

2. A favorite reward ____________________

1. ____________________ always helped clean the floor
and always was cheerful when doing a chore.
Though getting 2. ____________________ was sweet,
it wasn't for this 1. ____________________ would compete,
for working was like opening a door.

Tell you teacher three chores you do for your family.

1. ______________________________
2. ______________________________
3. ______________________________

Different Careers

1. Student's first name ______________________________

2. A word to describe something wonderful ______________________

1. ______________________________ was growing up here,

More each day it was perfectly clear.

So the future felt wondrous,

Like a 2. _______________________ traveling bus,

For soon 1. ______________________________ would have a career.

Color the bus below.

Flashcards

God's Scripture time

I can do all things through
Christ who strengthens me.

God's Scripture time

Fear not, for I
am with you . . .

God's Scripture time

And be kind to one another,
tenderhearted, forgiving one
another, even as God
in Christ forgave you.

God's Scripture time

I will praise You, for I am
fearfully and wonderfully
made; marvelous are Your
works, and that my soul
knows very well.

God's Scripture time

Isaiah 43:5

God's Scripture time

Philippians 4:13

God's Scripture time

Psalm 139:14

God's Scripture time

Ephesians 4:32

God's Scripture time

Rejoice in the Lord always.
Again I will say, rejoice!

God's Scripture time

You shall love your
neighbor as yourself.

God's Scripture time

For this is the love of God, that
we keep His commandments.
And His commandments
are not burdensome.

God's Scripture time

Trust in the LORD with all
your heart, and lean not on
your own understanding . . .

God's Scripture time

Matthew 22:39

God's Scripture time

Philippians 4:4

God's Scripture time 

Proverbs 3:5

God's Scripture time

1 John 5:3

God's Scripture time

And this is His commandment: that we should believe on the name of His Son Jesus Christ and love one another, as He gave us commandment.

God's Scripture time

God's Scripture time

God's Scripture time

God's Scripture time

1 John 3:23

God's Scripture time

God's Scripture time 

Language time 07:00

"Thank you" in Arabic

Language time 07:00

"Thank you" in Armenian

Language time 07:00

"Thank you" in Bosnian

Language time 07:00

"Thank you" in Bulgarian

Language time 07:00

"Thank you" in Bengali

Language time 07:00

"Thank you" in Cherokee

Language time 07:00

"Thank you" in Croatian

Language time 07:00

"Thank you" in Czech

Language time 07:00

Shnorhagallem
(snore hey gallem)

Language time 07:00

Shukran
(shoo crawn)

Language time 07:00

Blagodaria
(blah guh darria)

Language time 07:00

Hvala
(hvah lah)

Language time 07:00

Wado
(waw doe)

Language time 07:00

Dhanyabad
(doon yaw bawd)

Language time 07:00

Dekuji
(dye koo yih)

Language time 07:00

Hvala
(hvah lah)

Language time 07:00

"Thank you" in Dutch

Language time 07:00

"Thank you" in French

Language time 07:00

"Thank you" in German

Language time 07:00

"Thank you" in Hawaiian

Language time 07:00

"Thank you" in Hebrew

Language time 07:00

"Thank you" in Hindi

Language time 07:00

"Thank you" in Icelandic

Language time 07:00

"Thank you" in Indonesian

Language time 07:00

Merci
(mare see)

Language time 07:00

Dank u
(dawn koo)

Language time 07:00

Mahalo
(ma ha low)

Language time 07:00

Danke
(dawn ka)

Language time 07:00

Dhanyavad
(dawn ya vahd)

Language time 07:00

Todah
(toh dah)

Language time 07:00

Terima kasih
(tuh ree mah kah see)

Language time 07:00

Takk
(taw ck)

Language time 07:00

"Thank you" in Italian

Language time 07:00

"Thank you" in Japanese

Language time 07:00

"Thank you" in Korean

Language time 07:00

"Thank you" in Lithuanian

Language time 07:00

"Thank you" in Mandarin

Language time 07:00

"Thank you" in Norwegian

Language time 07:00

"Thank you" in Oriya

Language time 07:00

"Thank you" in Pashto

Language time 07:00

Arigato
(a ree gat oh)

Language time 07:00

Grazie
(graht tsyeh)

Language time 07:00

Achiu
(ah choo)

Language time 07:00

Kamsahamnida
(come sam nee dah)

Language time 07:00

Takk
(talk)

Language time 07:00

Xiexie
(shay shay)

Language time 07:00

Tashakor
(tash ah koor)

Language time 07:00

Dhanyabahd
(dun ya bawd)

Language time 07:00

"Thank you" in Quechua

Language time 07:00

"Thank you" in Russian

Language time 07:00

"Thank you" in Serbian

Language time 07:00

"Thank you" in Slovak

Language time 07:00

"Thank you" in Spanish

Language time 07:00

"Thank you" in Turkish

Language time 07:00

"Thank you" in Ukranian

Language time 07:00

"Thank you" in Vietnamese

Language time 07:00

Spasibo
(spy see bow)

Language time 07:00

Yusulpayki
(yoo sool pie key)

Language time 07:00

Dakujem
(jah koo yehm)

Language time 07:00

Hvala
(hvah lah)

Language time 07:00

Tesekkur ederim
(te shay kooreh dur um)

Language time 07:00

Gracias
(graw see us)

Language time 07:00

Cam on
(cam on)

Language time 07:00

Dyakuju
(jah coo joo)

Language time 07:00

"Thank you" in Welsh

Language time 07:00

"Thank you" in Xhosa

Language time 07:00

"Thank you" in Yoruba

Language time 07:00

"Thank you" in Zulu

MY STORY K
Name:
____

MY STORY K
Name:
____

MY STORY K
Name:
____

MY STORY K
Name:
____

Language time 07:00

Enkosi
(in co see)

Language time 07:00

Ngiyabona
(gee aw bone ah)

Language time 07:00

Diolch
(dee olich)

Language time 07:00

E se
(ee see)

word collector

Culture

word collector

Country

word collector

Holiday

word collector

Nutrition

word collector

Play

word collector

Uniform

A certain area of land ruled by a single government and known by other countries.

word collector

The language, art and music, and teachings of a group of people.

word collector

The act of eating good food and drinks to keep you healthy.

word collector

A special day to celebrate, made from the words "holy" and "day."

word collector

A kind of costume worn by people in a special group, like nurses or the police.

word collector

Activity that is fun and can help us learn as well.

word collector

Psalm

word collector

Words

word collector

Symbols

word collector

Character

word collector

Laws

word collector

Protect

Letters or sounds that mean something to people.

A special song that gives praise to God.

word collector

A word that tells us about who we are and how we act.

word collector

A picture that means something to people.

word collector

To try to keep someone from being hurt.

word collector

Rules to follow that are often created to keep us safe.

word collector

Traditions

word collector

Friends

word collector

Conflict

word collector

Leaders

word collector

Heroes

word collector

Citizen

word collector

People we like to spend time with who often like what we like.

A belief we act out and pass down to our families.

word collector

word collector

Those who lead people to be the best at whatever they do.

When we fight with our family or friends.

word collector

word collector

Someone who has special rights in their country.

People who work hard to make the world better and safer for others.

word collector

Neighbor

word collector

Maps

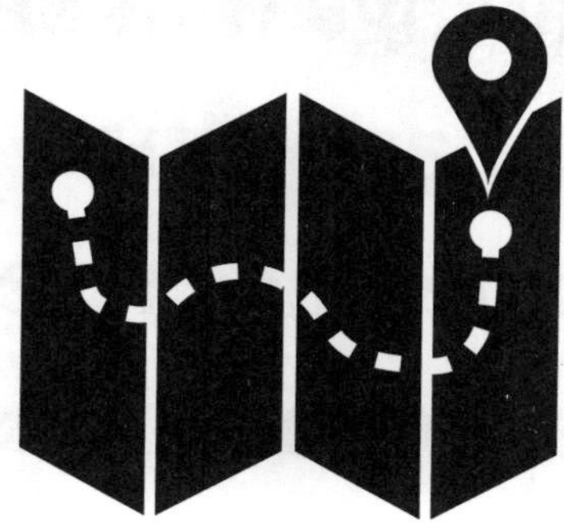

word collector

Community

word collector

Rural

word collector

Nationality

word collector

Timezones

Drawings that show roads and cities, and sometimes rivers and mountains.

word collector

A person who lives near our home.

word collector

A word that means out in the country, not in the city.

word collector

A group of people who live and work close together.

word collector

The earth is divided into 24 areas, or zones, where time is different.

word collector

Who you are because of the country where you were born.

word collector

Food

word collector

Geography

word collector

Weather

word collector

Needs

word collector

Wants

word collector

Purchase

A word that means writing about the earth.

word collector

What we eat to give us energy and keep us strong.

word collector

These are things we must have that we can't do without.

word collector

Different patterns of wind and water in the sky that make earth hot or cold.

word collector

To buy things from a person or a store.

word collector

These are things we would like to have but can live without.

word collector

Choices

word collector

Provides

word collector

Recycle

word collector

Services

word collector

Work

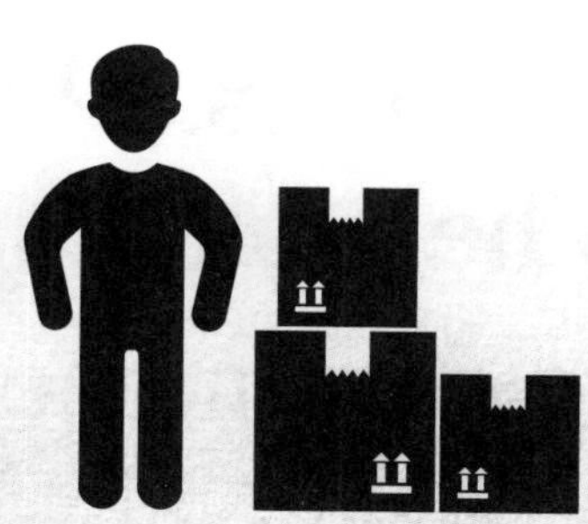

word collector

Career

Gives something to another, such as God providing all we need.

Picking between two or more things that we want or need.

Things people do for you that you pay them for (like a haircut).

word collector

To reuse so something is not wasted or thrown away.

word collector

A job you do over many years.

word collector

Something you do to help others or to earn money.

Canyon

A gorge or valley with rocky, sloped sides.

Cave

A tunnel or hollowed-out area underground, some with miles of connected passages.

Deserts

Deserts can be hot or cold, but they are most often dry places that receive less than 10 inches of rain each year.

Forest

There are three main kinds of forest, which are coniferous forests (forests with trees that have cones and needles), rain forests (forests with lots of rain and trees that never lose their leaves), and deciduous forests (forests with trees that lose their leaves in fall).

Grasslands

Grasslands are grassy areas found where there is too little rain for trees and more rain than a desert receives.

Hill

A mound of land raised above the surrounding landscape and smaller than a mountain.

Island

Islands are landforms surrounded by water.

Lake

A large body of fresh water enclosed by land.

Marsh

A low-lying wetland filled with diverse life and covered in tall grasses.

Mountains

Mountains are raised-up areas of land formed either by volcanic activity or movement on the earth's crust.

Ocean

Though the waters all flow together, there are five oceans recognized in the world. These are filled with salty water that is not drinkable, and much diverse life is designed to thrive here.

Reef (coral)

Made of limestone (calcium carbonate), reefs are formed when various algae, clams, corals, sponges, and other creatures cement themselves together in warm, shallow seas.

Rivers (brooks, creeks, streams)

These water sources are fed by rainfall and snowfall, transporting large amounts of water over hundreds and thousands of miles.

Valley

The lower areas between hills and mountains.

Volcano

A break in the ground that releases hot gas, ash, and lava from deep in the earth.

Waterfall

A stream or river that flows over a cliff, either as one drop (a cataract) or in sloped steps down a hill or mountain (a cascade).

Asia

1. Armenia
2. Bangladesh
3. China
4. India
5. Indonesia
6. Israel
7. Japan
8. Pakistan
9. Russia
10. South Korea
11. Thailand
12. Turkey
13. Vietnam

Africa

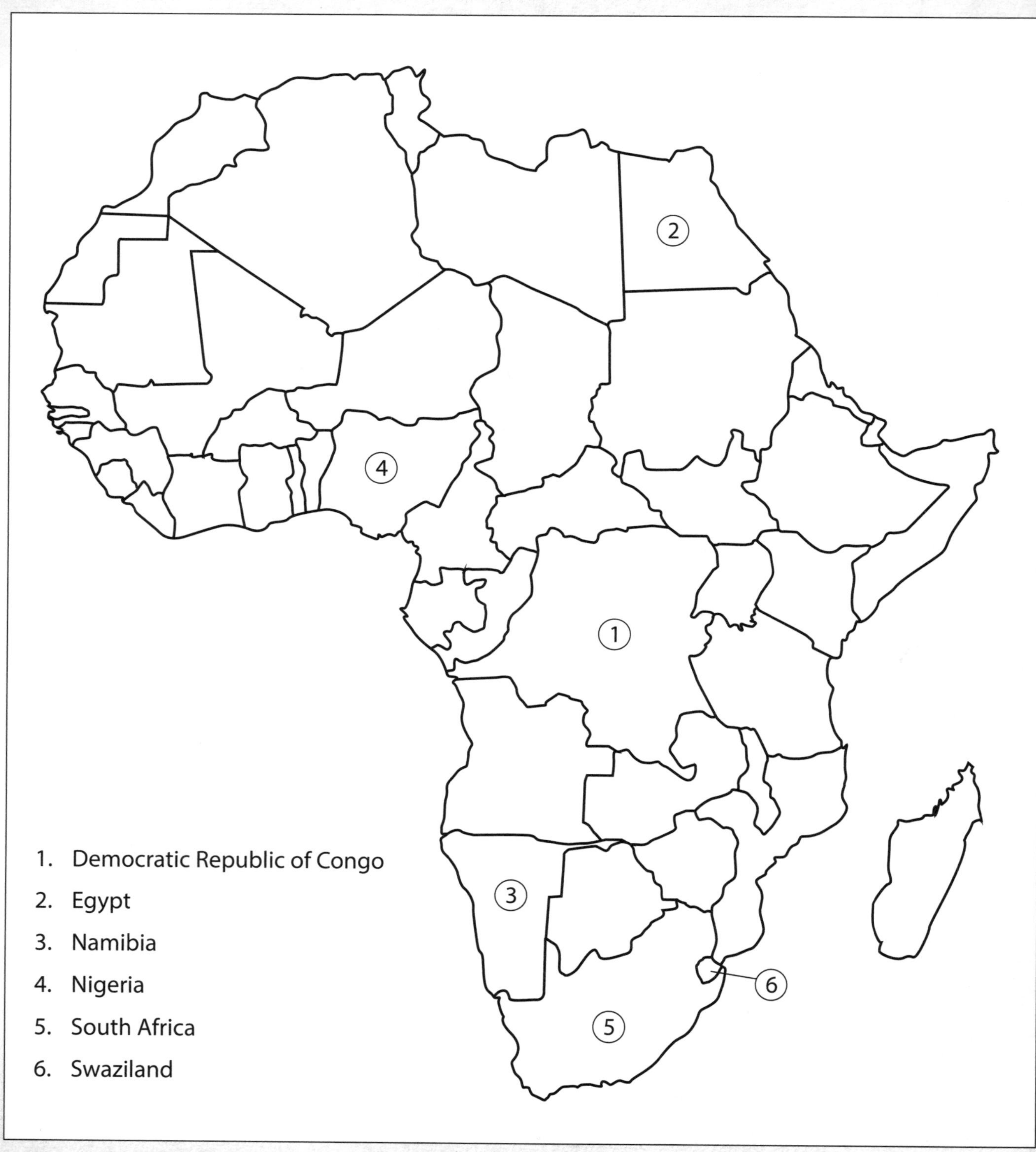

1
2
3
4
5
6
1. Democratic Republic of Congo
2. Egypt
3. Namibia
4. Nigeria
5. South Africa
6. Swaziland

North America

South America

Europe

1. Bosnia
2. Bulgaria
3. Croatia
4. Czech Republic
5. Iceland
6. Italy
7. Lithuania
8. Norway
9. Russia
10. Serbia
11. Slovakia
12. Ukraine
13. Wales

Australia/Oceania

Answers for Exercises

Page 65

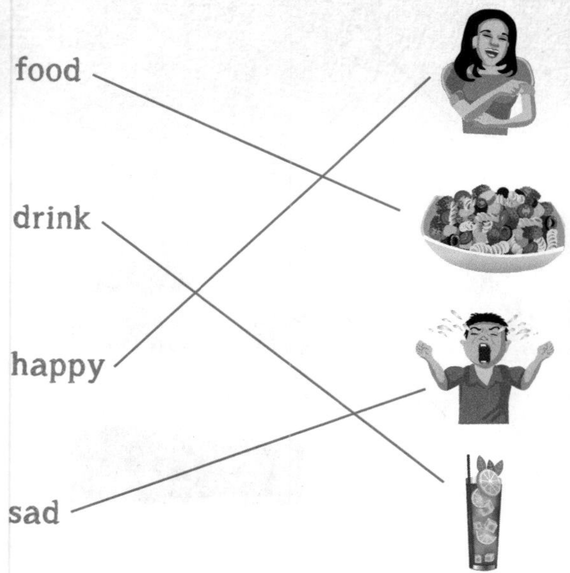

Page 121

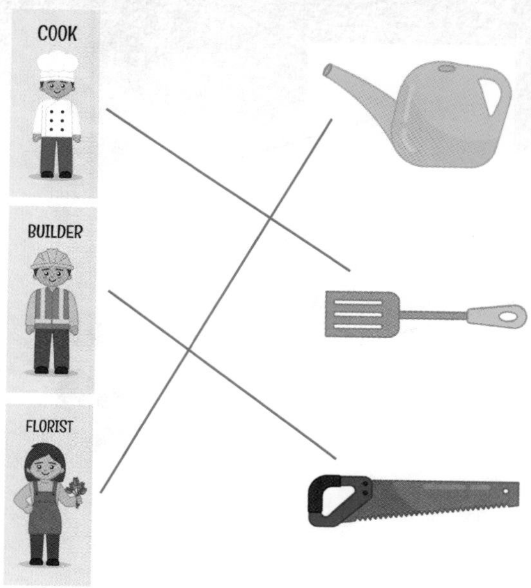

Page 115

Page 127

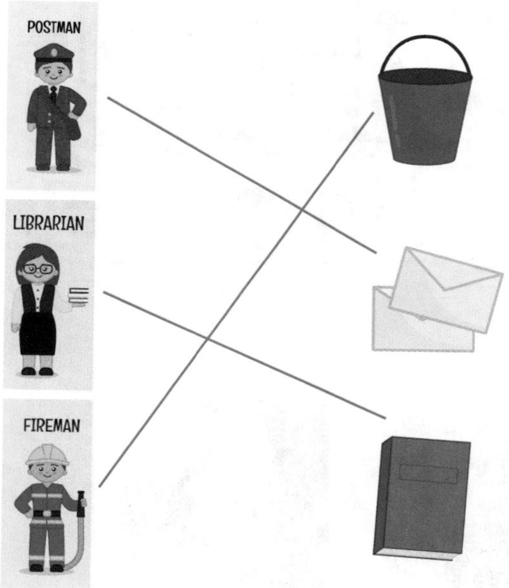

Page 133

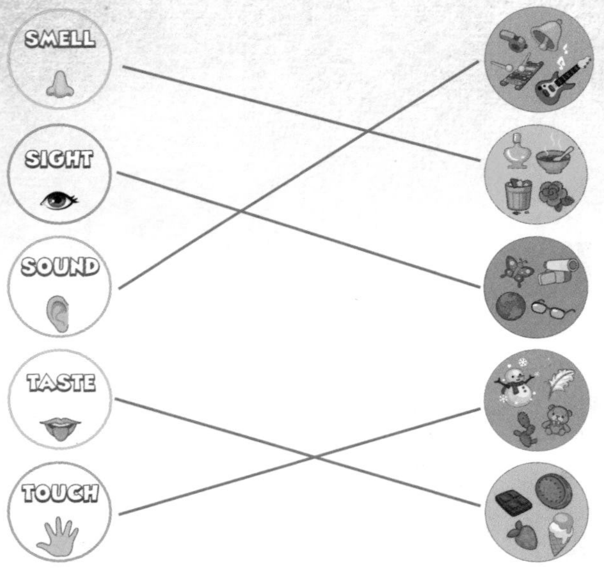

Page 151

Page 177

Page 191

Page 197

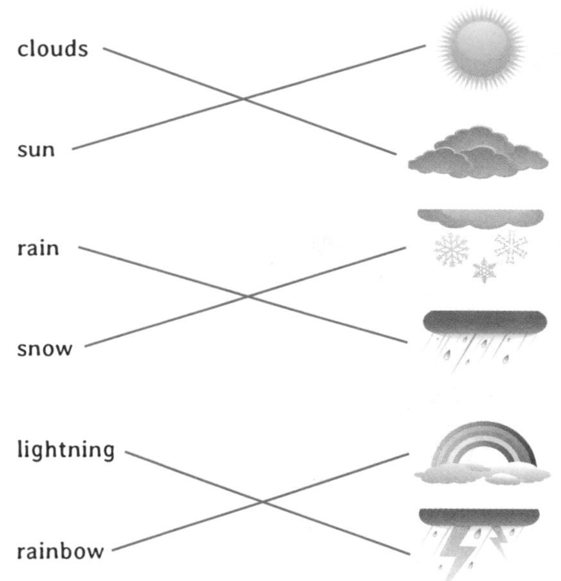

Page 213

Page 243

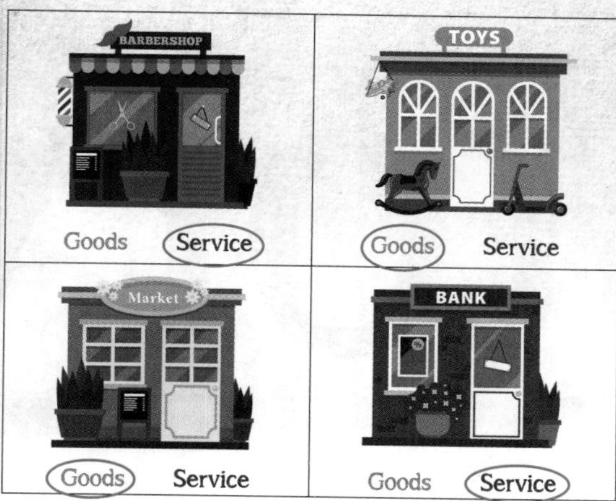

Page 245

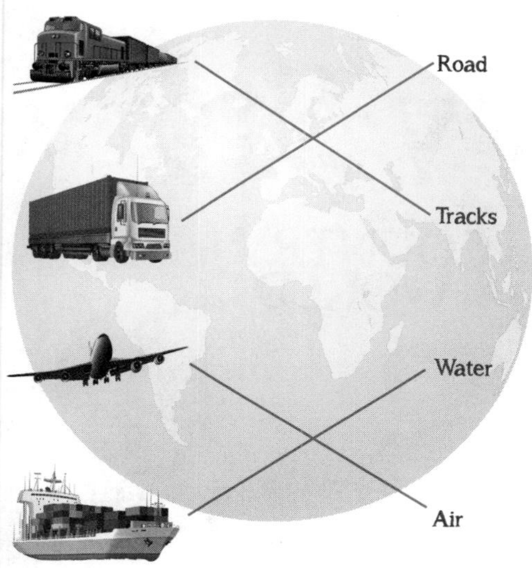

Page 257

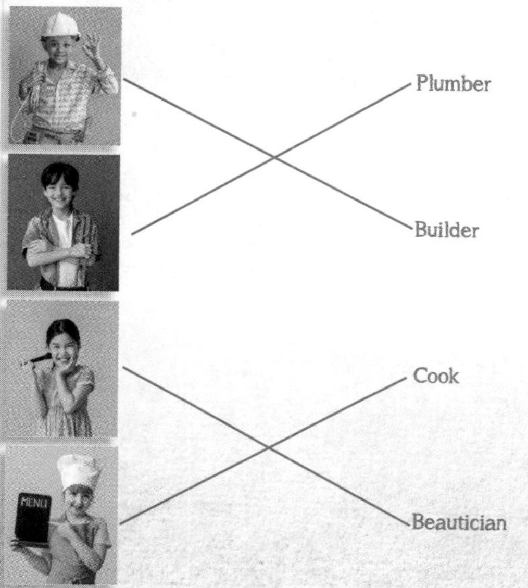

Page 284

My Story

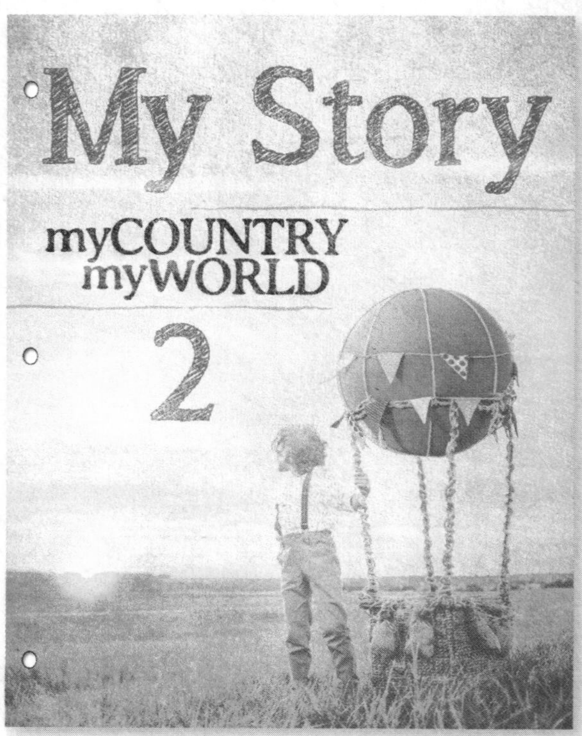

MY STORY 1

GRADE 1

This level one Social Studies curriculum begins with children in their homes, helping them think about their lives from their immediate families and beyond, as well as learning about local governments. Includes four quests.

9781683441175

MY STORY 2

GRADE 2

This level two Social Studies curriculum continues with a journey around the world, and lays a foundation for understanding state and federal governments, basic economic principles, and more. Four global quests included.

9781683441182